TWELVE SERMONS
ON
CONVERSION

TWELVE SERMONS
ON
CONVERSION

C. H. Spurgeon

BAKER BOOK HOUSE
Grand Rapids, Michigan

Paperback edition
issued by Baker Book House

ISBN: 0-8010-8027-4

First printing, July 1974
Second printing, January 1976
Third printing, June 1977

PHOTOLITHOPRINTED BY CUSHING - MALLOY, INC.
ANN ARBOR, MICHIGAN, UNITED STATES OF AMERICA
1977

CONTENTS

An Old-Fashioned Conversion

"Lo, all these things worketh God oftentimes with man, to bring back his soul from the pit, to be enlightened with the light of the living."—Job xxxiii. 29; 30.*

SOME people are wonderfully enamoured of anything that is old. An old coin, an old picture, an old book, or even a piece of antique rubbish, they will almost worship. The jingle of a rusty medal is music to them, and "auld nick-nackets" are as precious as diamonds. It is wonderful what a little mouldiness and a few worm-holes will do in the way of increasing values. I confess I do not very greatly share in the feeling, at least it is no craze of mine; but, nevertheless, all things being equal, antiquity has its charms. Old, old stories of the days far past, when time was young, have a special interest; they are as windows which permit us to gaze down the dim aisles of ages long gone by—we look through them with mingled curiosity and awe. I am about this morning to speak to you concerning an old conversion. We shall rehearse an ancient story of the renewal and salvation of a soul. In our day we meet with professors who cry down everything of the present, and cry up everything of the former days, which they call the good old times. Such persons talk much about old-fashioned conversions and hold in great admiration the lives of believers of the old school. I shall this morning introduce you to an old-fashioned conversion, and explain the way in which men were brought to God not only hundreds, but thousands of years ago. I suppose that Elihu delivered this description of conversion about the time of Moses, or at the period when Israel was in Egypt, for almost general consent appropriates one of those dates to the Book of Job. The record we shall read this morning, and study carefully, refers to the very very

---

* The real text is the whole passage from verse fourteen to thirty, and the reader is requested to turn to it before reading the sermon.

oldest times. Let this fact give additional interest to our meditation : and if it does I am sure that we shall not lack for earnest attention, for the subject is of great intrinsic value.

Kindly keep your Bibles open ; we have already read the chapter, but it will be needful to refer to it verse by verse.

I. The matter in hand is to compare an old-fashioned conversion with those of the present time, and the first note we shall strike is this : it is quite certain from the description given in this thirty-third chapter of Job that THE SUBJECTS OF CONVERSION WERE SIMILAR, and men in the far gone ages were precisely like men in these times. The passage tells us nothing about the stature of mens' bodies, but as far as they were spiritually concerned the photograph which Elihu took is the portrait of many of those who are brought to Jesus now. Reading the passage over, we find that men in those times needed converting ; for they were deaf to God's voice (verse 14) ; they were obstinate in evil purposes (verse 17), and puffed up with pride. They needed chastening to arouse them to thought, and required sore distress to make them cry out for mercy (verses 19—22). They were very loth to say, " I have sinned," and were not at all inclined to prayer. Nothing but sharp discipline could bring them to their senses, and even then they needed to be born again. Men in those days were sinful and yet proud ; sinful self and righteous self were both in power ; it was one part of conversion to withdraw them from their purposes of sin, and another part of their conversion to " hide pride " from them. Though they were sinful they thought that they were righteous, and though they were condemned by the law of God they still entertained the fond hope that they should by their own merits obtain the favour of the Most High. They were then, as they are now, poor as poverty and yet proud of their wealth, Publicans in sin, and yet Pharisees in boasting.

It appears that in those days God was accustomed to speak to men and to be disregarded by them ; we are told that God spake " once, yea, twice," and men perceived him not. Their presumptuous slumbers were too deep to be broken by the call of love. Samuel said, " Here am I, for thou didst call me," but they slept on in defiance of the Lord. O, how frequently doth the Lord speak now to deaf ears ! He calls, and men refuse, he stretches out his hands, and men do not regard him ; but they are desperately set upon their sins, and sodden in carnal security, therefore they do despite to his grace, and ruin their own souls.

In those ancient times, when a man was converted, the Lord himself must needs turn him, omnipotence itself was necessary to divide man from his folly. God's speaking to the ear was not enough unless he followed it up with a powerful application to the heart. Man was too far gone to be healed by remedies less than divine—he was utterly past hope unless Almighty love would come to the rescue ; verily the case is the same at this day, and each man repeats his fellow. As the fish still bites at the bait, as the bird still flies into the snare, as the beast is still taken in the pit, so is man still the dupe of his sins, and only the Lord can save him. Salvation was only wrought by the gracious influences of God's Spirit in the days of Job, and it is only so accomplished at this present hour. Men were lost then as now ; men thought they were not lost then, and they are equally conceited now. Into the house of the divine Physician the same class of persons enter as were welcomed and healed by him ages ago; he has the same blind eyes and deaf ears to open, hearts still require to be transformed from stone to flesh, and leprosies to be exchanged for health by his Sovereign touch. The Spirit from the four winds breathed on a valley covered with dry bones in the days of the fathers, and he comes forth still to work upon the like scene of death. Man has not outgrown his sins. As it was in the beginning it is now, and so it ever will be while that which is born of the flesh is flesh; as were the sires such are their sons, and such will our sons be in their turn; so that the process of conversion needs to be the same, and "all these things God worketh oftentimes with man."

II. The second note we shall strike is this, that in those olden times THE WORKER OF CONVERSION WAS THE SAME,—" *all these things God worketh.*" The whole process is by Elihu ascribed to God, and every Christian can bear witness that the Lord is the great worker now; he turns us, and we are turned. We read in verse fourteen, that at first the Lord wrought upon men by speaking to them, once, yea, twice: he also brought truth home to their minds and instructed them; and so changed their purposes and humbled their hearts. In the same manner the Lord worketh now. Conversion is a change which concerns the mind, the affections, the spirit; it is not a physical manipulation as some foolish persons fancy, who appear to think that God converts men by force, and turns them over as a man would roll a stone. The Lord operates upon men as men, not as blocks of wood; God speaks to them, instructs them, reveals truth to them, encourages them to hope, and graciously influences them for good. Man is left free, for " God speaketh once, yea, twice, yet man perceiveth it not," and yet in God's own wise and suitable manner, he is at length led to cry, " I have sinned and perverted that which is right, and it profited me not."

But in those times, as now, it was necessary that God should do more than speak to the outer ear, he therefore came nearer still, and by his Holy Spirit led men really to hear what he spake. He did not leave men to their wills, neither did he trust their conversion to the eloquence of preachers, or to the cogency of arguments, but he himself came and opened men's ears, and pressed the truth home upon their understandings, and made it operative upon their entire nature. Man was so proud that no one else could humble him but God; and he was so wilful, that no one could withdraw him from his purpose but the Lord alone: but the Lord in condescension did the deed, and made the man obedient and humble. Indeed, the Lord is described in this chapter as the main cause of all the work accomplished. Whereas, a ransom was needed to deliver men from going down to the pit, it is the Lord's voice which cried, " I have found a ransom." Whereas, even when the ransom was found, men did not know it, and would not receive it; it was God who sent a messenger, one of a thousand, to show unto man his uprightness, and to proclaim the great provision made for restoring man to his primeval state. It is the Lord who delivers the soul from the pit, that man's life may see the light.

In this chapter it is God that visits, that speaks, chastens, instructs, enlightens, consoles, renews and saves, from first to last. God worketh all in all. Salvation is of the Lord, it is not of man, neither by man; neither is it of the will of man, nor of the flesh, nor of blood, nor of birth, but of the will of God. The purpose of God and the power of God work salvation from first to last. What a blessing this is for us, for, if salvation were of ourselves, who among us would be saved? But he hath "laid help upon one that is mighty;" God also is our strength and our song, for he himself has become our salvation. He who has begun the good work will carry it on. Christ is the Alpha, and Christ is the Omega, the "author and the finisher of our faith." So we have two points in this ancient conversion in which it was just like our own, the same men to be operated upon, and the same God to work the miracles of grace.

III. The most interesting point to you will probably be the third: THE MEANS USED TO WORK CONVERSION IN THOSE DISTANT AGES WERE VERY MUCH THE SAME AS THOSE EMPLOYED NOW. There were differences in outward agencies, but the inward *modus operandi* was the same. There was a difference in the instruments, but the way of working was the same. Kindly turn to the chapter, at the fifteenth verse; you find there that God first of all spoke to men, but they regarded him not, and then he spoke to them effectually by means of a dream: "In a dream, in a vision of the night, when deep sleep falleth upon men, in slumberings upon the bed." Now, this was an extraordinary means of grace, seldom used now. In this the distant ages differ from the present. A dream, though it be in itself but the phantasm of sleep, may be employed by God to arouse the mind towards eternal things. Dreams of death and judgment to come have frequently had a very alarming effect upon the conscience, while visions of celestial glory have impressed the heart with desires after infinite bliss. As Dryden says of some men—

> "In sleep they fearful precipices tread;
> Or, shipwreck'd, labour to some distant shore,"

so others have in their slumbers shivered at the gates of hell, or even been tossed upon its fiery waves, and the thoughts consequent upon such dreams have, by God's grace, occasionally been rendered permanently useful, though I fear it is not often so. In the days of Elihu, however, dreams were much more frequently the way in which God spake, for there were few messengers from God to interpret his mind, no openly declared gospel, and few assemblies for instruction by hearing the word; and what is more, there was then no written word of God. In those early times they had no inspired books at all, so that, lacking the Bible, and lacking the frequent ministrations of God's servants, the Lord was pleased to supply their deficiencies by speaking to men in the visions of the night. I say again, we must not expect the Lord to return to the general use of so feeble an agency now that he employs others which are far more effectual. It is much more profitable for you to have the word in your houses which you can read at all times, and to have God's ministers to proclaim clearly the gospel of Jesus, than it would be to be dependent upon visions of the night.

The means, therefore, outwardly, may have changed, but still, whether it be by the dream at night, or by the sermon on the Sabbath, the power is just the same : namely, in the word of God. God speaks to men in dreams, if so, he speaks to them all nothing more and nothing different from what he speaks in the written word. If any come to you and say, " I have dreamed this or that," and it be not in the Scriptures, away with their dreams ! If anything should occur in your own mind in vision which is not already revealed in the Book of God, put it away, it is an idle fancy not to be regarded. Woe to that man whose religion is the baseless fabric of dreams, he will one day wake up to find that nothing short of realities could save him. We have the more sure word of testimony, unto which we do well if we take heed as unto a light that shineth in a dark place. Conversions, then, in the old time, used to be by the word of God ; it came in a different way, but it was the same word and the same truth. At this time faith cometh by hearing, and hearing by the word of God, and at bottom that was precisely the way in which faith came to men in those distant periods.

Now, observe, that in addition to the external coming of the word, it seems from the chapter before us in the sixteenth verse, that men were converted by having their ears opened by God. Alas, men's ears are still stopped up ! An old Puritan has mentioned seven forms of what he calls " ear stoppers," which need to be taken out of the human ear. They are frequently blocked up by ignorance ; they know not the importance and value of the truth, and, therefore they refuse to give earnest heed to it ; judging it to be an idle tale, they go their ways to their farms and to their merchandise. Some ears are stopped up by unbelief ; they have heard the glad tidings of salvation, but they have not received it as an infallible revelation from heaven, a message backed by divine authority. Scepticism and philosophy, falsely so called, barricade Ear-gate against the assaults of Emmanuel's captains, so that even the great battering-rams of the gospel prove powerless to force an entrance. " He could not do many mighty works then because of their unbelief ! " Others ears are stopped up by impenitence ; the hardness of the heart causes a deadness of the ear. You may discharge the great cannons of the law in the ears of some men, but they will not stir ; the thunders of God startle the wild beasts of the wood, but impenitence is not moved thereby. The gospel itself soundeth upon such ears with no more effect than upon a marble statue ; the groans of Calvary are nothing to them. Some ears are stopped by prejudice ; they have made up their minds as to what the gospel ought to be, and they will not hear it as it is ; they have set up for themselves a standard of what the truth should be, and that standard is a false one, for they have put bitter for sweet and sweet for bitter, darkness for light and light for darkness. Prejudices against the preacher, or against the denomination are but forms of the same evil ; they make men to be as Ulysses was when his ears were sealed with wax, for they are even as deaf men. The entrance into many ears is also effectually barred by the love of sin. He who loves vice will not hear of repentance ; the lover of pleasure detests holy mourning ; the licentious think holiness to be another name for slavery. The man who finds delight in sin is a deaf adder whom the wisest charmer cannot charm ; the poison of asps is under his tongue, and he cannot renounce his deadly hate of a gospel which rebukes his evil ways. It would be vain to teach cleanliness to the sow which wallows in the mire—it loves uncleanness, and after uncleanness will it go. Some ears are stopped through pride ; the plain, unflattering, humbling gospel of the sinner's Saviour is not to their taste. The gospel for lost sinners, they think, is not addressed to them, for they are almost good enough, and are by no means worthy of any great blame, or in danger of any great punishment. When they acknowledge their sinnership in words they feel it not in their hearts, therefore they hear not the truth in the love of it. If the gospel-pipe could be tuned to notes of flattery, to praise the dignity of man, they would attend to its music, but a gospel for vulgar sinners ! How can their noble souls endure it ? With their fine feathers all ruffled in disdain, they turn away in a rage. Alas ! how many ears are stopped through worldliness ! If you stand in a street where the traffic is abundant—where the constant thunder of rumbling wheels creates a din—it would be difficult to preach so as to command an audience, for the abundant sound would prevent all hearing ; and, to a great extent, the mass of mankind are just in that position as to the joyful sound of the gospel ; the rumbling of the wheels of commerce, the noise of trade and the cries of competition, the whirl of cares and the riot of pleasures—all these drown the persuasive voice of heavenly love, so that men hear no more of it than they would hear a pin fall in the midst of a hurricane at sea. Only when God unstops the ear is the still small voice of truth heard in the chambers of the heart.

Now it is clear to every thoughtful person that all these ear-stoppers existed in the olden times as well as now, and therefore the same work of opening the passage to the heart was necessarily performed. Dreams did not convert sinners of the patriarchal age, however vivid they might be, nor did prophetic warnings by themselves arouse them,—the hand of him who created the ear was needed to cleanse and circumcise it, ere the truth could find admission.

Note the next sentence, he " sealeth their instruction." That was the means of conversion in the olden times. God brought the truth down upon the soul as you press a seal upon the wax : you bear upon the seal to make the impress, and even thus the power of God pressed home the word. Truth is heard by men, but they forget it unless the Holy Spirit takes the truth and puts it home, and lays his force upon it, and then it makes a stamp upon the conscience, upon the memory, and upon the entire manhood. Perhaps, also, by sealing here is meant confirming. A thing is sealed when it is established by testimony and witness : under hand and seal as we say. Now the Holy Spirit has a way of making truth to become manifest to men, and cogent upon their minds by bearing his witness with it ; so that they cannot help feeling that it is true. He sets it in such a light, that they cannot dispute it, but yield full consent to it, their conscience being overwhelmingly convinced.

Dear friends, I pray God the Holy Spirit in this sense to seal home the word we speak to each one of you, that from hearers you may grow into believers. I know you will remain hearers only unless that sacred sealing shall take place ; but let that come upon you and your soul will bear the gospel stamped into its very texture, never more to be effaced. If the Spirit of God thus seals you, you will be sealed indeed.

By sealing is also sometimes meant preserving and setting apart, as we seal up documents or treasures of great value, that they may be secure. In this sense the gospel needs sealing up in our hearts. We forget what we hear till God the Holy Ghost seals it in the soul, and then it is pondered and treasured up in the heart : it becomes to us a goodly pearl, a divine secret, a peculiar heritage. This sealing is a main point in conversion. What thousands of sermons many of you have heard, but the instruction has never been sealed to you, and, therefore, you remain unsaved. I cannot bear to think of your unhappy case, and I beseech those who love the Lord to pray that our discourses, or the sermons of some one else, or the Bible itself, may be sealed of the Lord upon these my unhappy hearers, that they may be converted and saved. O for the Lord's sealing hand upon men's hearts ! Send, Lord, by whomsoever thou wilt send, and by thy servant also. Give the hearing ear, and then engrave thy gospel upon an understanding heart. Thou art able to do this, and in faith we seek it at thy hands, O Lord God of our salvation. In this manner men were converted in the olden times : ears were opened and hearts were sealed.

It appears, also, that the Lord, in those days, employed providence as a help towards conversion—and that providence was often of a very gentle kind, for it preserved men from death. Read the eighteenth verse :—" He keepeth back his soul from the pit, and his life from perishing by the sword." Many a man has had the current of his life entirely changed by an escape from imminent peril ; solemn thoughts have taken possession of his formerly careless mind, and he has said to himself, " Has God preserved me from this danger, then let me be grateful to him. He must have had a purpose in my preservation, let me find out what it is, and thankfully endeavour to answer to it." Have any of you, my hearers, escaped from shipwreck ? Is there one here who has escaped from accident upon the iron way ? Are you one of a handful who were snatched from between the very jaws of death ? Have you risen up from a fever which laid you very low ? Are you now almost the only survivor of a family, all the members of which, except yourself, have been taken away by consumption, or some other hereditary disease ? Are you a remarkable monument of sparing mercy ? Then, I pray you, let the long-suffering of God lead you to repentance, for it has led many before you, and it is intended that it should do the like for you. Yield to the gentle pressure of lovingkindness, even as the flowers yield their perfumes to the sunshine : do not need to be crushed and bruised like Oriental spice beneath the pestle. Tenderly doth the Lord call you to himself, and say, " I have spared thee from the grave, I have also kept thy guilty soul from going down to hell, I have placed thee to-day under the sound of the gospel ; I am, by my servant, calling upon thee to turn unto me and live. Wilt thou not hear me ? Thou art still on praying ground and pleading terms with me—wilt thou not consider all this ? " Thus God speaketh now by actions, which speak more loudly than words, and it seems that in the same way he was wont to speak to men in the days gone by, so that providential circumstances were often the means of conversion.

But, further, it seems that, as Elihu puts it, sickness was a yet more effectual awakener in the common run of cases. Observe the nineteenth verse, "He is chastened also with pain upon his bed, and the multitude of his bones with strong pain : so that his life abhorreth bread, and his soul dainty meat." Severe pain destroyed appetite and brought on extreme lassitude and distaste of life : but all this was sent in mercy to fetch the wanderer home. Yes, men get space for thought when they are shut up in the chamber of sickness. While the mill-wheel went on and on and on, they could not hear God speak, but when its hum is hushed the warning voice sounds forth clearly. There in silence the patient tosses on the bed, wakeful at night, and fearful by day, and then conscience lifts up its clamour and will be heard : then, too, the Spirit of God seizes the opportunity to speak to an awakened conscience, and he convinces the man of sin. How much some of us owe to a bed of sickness ! I do not desire for any unconverted person here that he should be ill, but if that would be the way to make him think, repent, and believe, I could earnestly pray for it. I believe the Lord has often preached to men in hospitals who never heard him in churches or chapels ; fever and cholera have been heard by those whom ministers could not reach. If we could banish pain and sickness from the world, it may be we should be robbing righteousness of two of her most impressive evangelists. What Jonah was to Nineveh, sickness has been to many a man. Like Elijah also, it has cried in the soul, "Choose ye this day whom ye will serve." Disease has been a grim orator for God, and with an eloquence not to be resisted, it has made the hearts of men to bow before its message. If there are any here who have lately been thus afflicted, I would ask them whether God has blessed it to their souls. I earnestly pray that they may not be hardened by it, for in that case there is fear that God will say, "Why should ye be smitten any more, ye will revolt more and more !" and he may add, "I will let them alone, they are given unto idols. I have smitten them till their whole head is sick, and their whole heart is faint. I have made them to be so near death's door, that from the crown of the head even to the foot they are all wounds and bruises through the chastenings of my rod. I will give them up, and no more will I deal with them in a way of grace." Great God have pity still, and make thy chastisements effectual to their souls. Now, note well that we do not assert that all persons who are saved are awakened by sickness ; far from it, all that we are now taught is that many are so aroused, and that such was the case in the instance described by Elihu.

In addition to this sickness, the person whom God saved was even brought to be apprehensive of death—"Yea, his soul draweth near unto the grave, and his life to the destroyers." When a man is made to lie upon his bed on the brink of hell and look into another world, that sight may be sacredly blessed to him. O, it is no small thing to peer into eternity, and to make out, amid the horrid gloom, no shapes of hope but ghastly forms of hideous woe. To have behind one the memory of a mis-spent life, to have above one an angry God, to have within one the aches of the body and the pangs of remorse, and to have beneath one the bottomless pit, yawning with its lurid fires! What can be worse? This side of hell, what can be worse than the tortures of an awakened conscience? This has sometimes made men wake up from a life-slumber and compelled them to cry, "What must we do to be saved?" I could wish that every man here, who has remained unmoved by gentler means, might have some such an experience. It were better for you to be saved so, as by fire, than not to be saved at all.

But, now, notice that all this did not lead the person into comfort ; although he was impressed by the dream and sickness, and so on, yet the ministry of some God-sent ambassador was wanted. "If there be a messenger with him," that is a man sent of God—"an interpreter," one who can open up obscure things and translate God's mind into man's language—"one among a thousand," for a true preacher, expert in dealing with souls, is a rare person "to show unto man his uprightness, then he is gracious unto him." God could save souls without ministers, but he does not often do it ; he could bring men to Jesus without the call from the lip of his sent servants, but as a general rule conversion in the olden times needed the messenger and the interpreter, and it needs them still : "How shall they believe on him of whom they have not heard, and how shall they hear without a preacher, and how shall they preach except they be sent." I pray that many of you, dear brethren, who know the Lord, may become preachers to others ; that you may be such successful messengers of mercy to poor broken hearts, that you may be to them picked and choice men like one out of a thousand. I entreat you to pray for me also, that I may have a share, and a large share, in this blessed employment, and that to many God may say through me, "Deliver him from going down to the pit, for I have found a ransom."

IV. Fourthly, and with too much brevity, THE OBJECTS AIMED AT IN THE OLD CONVERSIONS WERE JUST THE SAME as those that are aimed at now-a-days. Will you kindly look at the seventeenth verse. The first thing that God had to do with the man was to withdraw him from his purpose. He finds him set upon sin, upon rebellion, upon carnal pleasure, upon everything that is selfish and worldly ; and conversion turns him away from such evil purposes : it was so then, it is so now. This turning of an obstinate will towards God and holiness is, however, no easy matter : to stay the sun in his course, or reverse the marches of the moon, would not be a harder task.

The next object of the divine work was to hide pride from man, for man will stick to self-righteousness as long as he can. Never does limpet adhere to its rock more firmly than a sinner to his own merits, although indeed he has none. Like the old Greek hero in the mythology, the natural man sits down upon the stone of self-esteem, and Hercules himself cannot tear him from it. When he is even in outward character vile, he still fancies that there is some good thing in him, and to that fancy he will tenaciously cling ; so that it is a work of divine power, an effort of the august omnipotence of heaven, to get a man away from his innate and desperate pride.

Beloved, another great object of conversion is to lead man to a confession of his sin. Hence we find it said in the twenty-seventh verse,

" He looketh upon man, and if any say I have sinned, and perverted that which was right, and it profited me not, he will deliver his soul from going into the pit." Man hates confession to his God, I mean humble, personal, hearty confession. He will go to a priest and answer all his filthy questions, but he will not confess to the Lord. He will gabble over words which he calls a " general confession," but true, heart-felt confession he shrinks from—he will not come to the publican's cry if he can help it. He will not say, frankly from his heart, " I have sinned." He will not own or confess the perverseness of his nature and say, " I have perverted that which is right ;" nor can you get him to own the folly and stupidity of his sin, so as to say, " it profited me not." But conversion brings him to his knees, conversion pulls up the sluices of his soul, and makes him pour out his confessions before the Most High ; and when this is done, then salvation has come to the man's soul, for God desires man to put himself into the place of condemnation in order that he may be able to say to him, " I forgive thee freely." The Lord shuts us up to hopelessness and helplessness in order that he may come, as a God of grace, and display his abounding mercy. All our hope lies in him, and all other hopes are delusions. The great work in con-version is not to make people better, so that they may come to God on a good footing, it is to strip them completely and lay them low, so that God may come to them when they are on a bad footing, or rather on no footing at all, but down in the dust at his feet. The Son of man is come to seek and to save that which is lost, but it wants God himself to convince men that they are lost ; and the Spirit's work of soul-humbling is just this,—to get man to feel so diseased that he will accept the physician ; to get him to feel so poor that he will accept the charity of heaven ; to get him to know that he is so stripped, that he will no longer be proud of his fig leaves, but will be willing to take the robe of righteousness which Christ has wrought out. Conviction is sent to kill the man, to break him in pieces, to bury him, to let him know his own corruption ; and all this as a preliminary to his quickening and restoration. We must see the bones in the valley to be dead and dry, or we shall not hear the voice out of the excellent glory, saying, " Thus saith the Lord, ' Ye dry bones live ! ' " May God in his mercy teach us what all this means ; and may we all experience an old-fashioned conversion.

V. Fifthly, the process of conversion in days of yore exactly resembled that which is wrought in us now as to ITS SHADES. The shadowy side wore the same sombre hues as now. First of all, the man refused to hear ; God spake once, yea twice, and man regarded him not : here was obstinate rebellion. His heart was as an adamant stone. How true is that to-day ! Then came the chastening till the man's bones were made to ache, and he was full of misery. It is often the same now. I acknowledge that I was brought to God by agony of soul. I have often said from this pulpit that no man ever steers his barque towards the port of peace till he is driven there by stress of weather. We never come to Christ till we feel we cannot do without him. We must feel our poverty before we shall ever come and beg at the door of his mercy for help. The shades are the same, for the same imminence of danger which Elihu spoke of comes upon every sinner's consciousness, more or less before he resorts to Jesus for refuge. The same bitter sense of sin comes over men still, and the same wonder at their own folly in having continued in it. The same darkness still covers the sinner's pathway, and the same inability to procure the light for himself; the same need of light from above, the same need of help from him who is mighty to save. If any of you are passing just now through great darkness of soul, because you have not yet come to the light, but God is revealing yourselves to yourselves, be comforted, for the same dark road has been traversed by many of the saints before you, and it is a safe pathway, leading to comfort in Jesus Christ.

VI. But now, sixthly and very briefly, again, THE LIGHTS ARE THE SAME, even as the shades were the same. You will note in Elihu's description, that the great source of all the light was this :—" Deliver him from going down to the pit, for I have found a ransom." There is not a gleam of light in the case till you come to that divine word,— and is it not so now? Did you ever get any comfort for your troubled souls till you were led to see the ransom found by God in Jesus Christ? Did you ever know the value of the ransom for yourselves till God spoke it home to you—" Deliver *him* from going down to the pit, for *I* have found a ransom! " This is the central point of the sinner's hope—a bleeding Saviour paying our ransom price in drops of blood, the dying Son of God achieving our redemption by his own death. Oh, dear souls, who are in the dark, if you want light, there is light nowhere but at the cross. Do not look within for light ; the only benefit of looking within is to be more and more convinced that all is dark as midnight apart from Jesus. Look within if you want to despair, but if you wish for hope, look yonder to Calvary's mountain, where the Son of God lays down his life that sinners may not die. Hear you from heaven the voice which saith, " I have found a ransom." That is the only reason why God delivers you, not because he has seen any good thing in you, but because he has found a ransom for you. Look where God looks, and your comfort will begin.

Then this precious gospel being announced to the sinner, the comfort of it enters his soul in the exercise of prayer :—" He shall pray unto God, and he will be favourable unto him." O, you can pray when you get to the cross ; our prayers, before we see Christ, are poor poor things, but when we get to Calvary, and see the utmost ransom paid, and the full atonement made, then prayer becomes the utterance of a child to a father, and we feel quite sure it will speed.

Next, it appears, that the soul obtains comfort because God gave it his righteousness—" for he will render unto man his righteousness." That righteousness which God expected God bestows ; that righteousness which man ought to have wrought out but could not, Christ works out ; and God treats the believing man as if he were righteous, making him righteous in the righteousness of Christ. Here is another source of joy.

And then the man being led to a full confession of his sin in the twenty-seventh verse, the last cloud upon his spirit is blown away and he is at perfect peace. God was gracious to the man described by Elihu. God himself became his light and his salvation, and he came forth into joy and liberty. There is nothing more full of freshness and surprise than the joy of a new convert. Though thousands have felt it, yet each one as he feels it is himself amazed. I did really think when God forgave me that I was the most extraordinary instance of his Sovereign love that ever lived, and that I should be bound even in heaven itself to tell to others how God's infinite mercy had pardoned in my case the biggest sinner that ever was forgiven, Now, every saved soul is led to feel just that, and to exult and rejoice, and magnify the Lord with extreme surprise, because of his goodness. It seems it was so in Job's day, and it is so now ; the old conversions are the conversions of the period : the shades are the same and the lights are the same.

VII. And last of all, which is the seventh point, THE RESULTS ARE THE SAME, for I think I hardly know a better description of the result of regeneration than that which is given in the twenty-fifth verse : " His flesh shall be fresher than a child's : he shall return to the days of his youth." He who was an old wrinkled man in sin, and looked yet older through his sorrow, becomes born again, starts upon a new career with a new life within him ; the health which had departed from his soul comes back, the spring of spiritual juvenility wells up in him, because God has begotten him afresh and made him a new creature : " Old things have passed away, behold all things are become new ! "

And with this change comes back joy. See the twenty-sixth verse : " He shall see his face with joy ; for he will render unto man his righteousness ;" and the thirtieth verse : "To bring back his soul from the pit, to be enlightened with the light of the living." So that the new spirit finds itself in a new world, in which it goeth forth with joy and is led forth with peace ; the mountains and the hills break forth before it into singing, and all the trees of the wood do clap their hands. It was so then ; it is just the same now. O that the same blessed thing may happen to many here present at this time !

I have endeavoured to give a description of conversion, that you may see what it is to be renewed in heart, but I shall have failed of my intention unless many a knee shall be bent to God with this prayer, " O Spirit of God, renew my nature, change my heart : make my flesh to be fresher than a child's, make me a new creature in Christ Jesus." Time is passing : we are getting now almost one-fourth through another year, and the year itself will soon fly away. I would speak to careless and thoughtless ones again, and ask them will it never be time to think upon these things ? Will it never be time to consider your ways ? Will it never be time to seek unto the Lord ? Ye know not how near ye are to the grave's brink. Do consider, I beseech you, and remember that the Lord waiteth to be gracious, that he delighteth in mercy, and if you seek him he will be found of you ; and this great conversion and regeneration, of which we have spoken at such length, shall be yours, and you shall see the face of God with joy even as they did of old. The Lord grant it to you for the Redeemer's sake. Amen.

Conversions Desired

"And the hand of the Lord was with them: and a great number believed, and turned unto the Lord."—Acts xi. 21.

THE brethren who had dwelt together in church fellowship at Jerusalem were scattered abroad by persecution which arose about Stephen. Their Master had told them that when they were persecuted in one city they were to flee to another. They obeyed his command, and in the course of escape from persecution they took very long journeys—very long journeys indeed for that age of the world, when locomotion was exceedingly difficult: but wherever they found themselves they began at once to preach Jesus Christ, so that the scattering of the disciples was also a scattering of good seed in broader fields. The malice of Satan was made the instrument of the mercy of God. Learn from this, dear brethren, every one of you, that wherever you are called to go you should persevere in making known the name and gospel of Jesus. Look upon this as your calling and occupation. You will not be scattered now by persecution, but should the demands of business carry you into different climes, employ your distant travel for missionary purposes. Providence every now and then bids you remove your tent, take care that wherever it is pitched you carry with you a testimony for Jesus. At times the necessities of health require relaxation and change of air, and this may take you to different places of public resort: seize the opportunity to encourage the churches in such localities by your presence and countenance, and also endeavour to spread the knowledge of Jesus among those to whom you may be directed. The position which you occupy in society is not an accidental one; it has not been decreed to you by a blind, purposeless fate; there is predestination in it, but that predestination is wise, and looks towards a merciful end: you are placed where you are that you may be a preserving salt to those around, a sweet savour of Christ to all who know you. The methods of divine grace have ordained a happy connection between you and the people with whom you associate; you are a messenger of mercy to them, a herald of good tidings, an epistle of Christ. The surrounding darkness needs you, and therefore it is written, "Among whom ye shine as lights in the world." You are intended to warn and rebuke some, to entreat and encourage others. To you the mourner looks for comfort and the ignorant for instruction; let them never look in vain. Be the true friend of men, observe their condition before God, and endeavour to reclaim them from their wanderings. If Joseph was sent to Egypt that he might save his father's house alive, you also are sent where you are for the sake of some hidden ones of the Lord's chosen family. If Esther was placed in the court of a heathen king for the deliverance of her nation, so are you, my sister, called to occupy your present position for the good of the church of Christ. Look ye to it, brethren, lest ye miss your life's object, and live in vain. It would be a sad thing indeed if you who profess to belong to Christ should be "creation's blot, creation's blank," by having failed to work while it is called to-day.

These good people of the early church, however, with all their zeal, were somewhat narrow-minded and hampered by their national preju- dices, for they preached at first to the Jews only, and it was very hard to make them see that the gospel was meant for the whole race of man, Gentiles as well as Jews. Their Master had said "Go ye into all the world, and preach the gospel to every creature," and yet they began with preaching to the Jews only. Words could not have been plainer, and yet they missed their meaning. It is not to be wondered at that some in our day are still unable to preach to men as men when we see how slow the early saints were to learn the lesson. Brethren, if there be any narrowness about our spirit, let us pray the Lord to take it away. We shall not, of course, be shackled as these Jews were by boasting our nationality, but perhaps there may be classes of society of whom we despair, and therefore for whom we make no effort. We say, "It would be useless to attempt the conversion of such characters. I feel myself quite able to talk to other persons; but although I am placed in the midst of these people I cannot bring my mind to speak with them about spiritual things, for I feel hopeless of success." Beloved, may you be delivered from this snare, and learn to sow beside all waters. The Gentiles, though they were for awhile passed over by the brethren, turned out to be the most hopeful of all classes; from the Gentile fields they reaped harvests such as were never gathered in Judea. Antioch with its Grecians became famous among Christian churches—there the church of Christ first took its name amid a revival of religion, when great multitudes believed and turned unto the Lord. God had from of old intended that the great majority of the election of grace should be gathered out of those very Gentiles whom even the apostles themselves scarcely ventured to address. Now then, my brother, in the light of this incident begin to work where as yet you have done nothing: begin to hope where hitherto you have despaired, throw out your best energies in that very direction in which you have felt most hampered, for there awaits you, to your own intense surprise, a success which will amply reward you. You need not restrict yourselves to lands familiar with the plough, invade the primeval forest, fell the ancient trees, and clear the broad acres : that virgin soil will yield you harvests a hundredfold such as you will never find in fields where others have laboured before you. If your spiritual mining is becoming a failure, open fresh lodes of the precious metal, for veins of treasure lie concealed in the unbroken ground. Launch out into the deep, and let down your nets for a draught, and multitudes of fish shall crowd the net. It seems to me to be the obvious teaching of the text that wherever we are cast we should try to do good, and that we may hope for the largest success among the most neglected portions of society.

Coming closely to the text, I desire to press upon you this morning, with great earnestness, the need of the conversion of men, and the desirableness that we should have many converted here, and I shall want to suggest what we can do to produce that result. In all these I beg to be assisted by the Holy Spirit, without whose aid I shall only exhibit my own weakness, and deaden those energies which I long to arouse. These will be our heads : first, *the end we aim at,* that many may believe and turn unto the Lord ; secondly, *the power by which this can be attained,* " The hand of the Lord was with them "; thirdly, *the desirableness of our object;* and, fourthly, *how we may promote its attainment.*

I. Let us speak upon THE END WHICH WE DESIRE. It may seem very commonplace, but it is in fact one of the grandest designs under heaven : he who contemplates it has a higher aim than philosopher, reformer, or patriot. He aims at that for which the Son of God both lived and died. We desire that men may believe, that is to say, first, *that they may believe the testimony of Jesus Christ to be true,* for there are some who have not reached as far as that : they reject altogether the inspired Word, and to them the incarnation, the redemption, the resurrection, the glory, the second advent, are so many old wives' fables. You to whom these truths are the light of your lives can scarcely realise the power of unbelief of this kind, and yet some men live and die in its gloom. We pray that they may be taught better, and that the evidence of these great facts may be forced home upon them. Alas, there are many who profess to believe these things, but their only reason for so doing is that they have been taught so from their childhood, and it is the current religion of the nation. They regard the inspiration of Scripture, and so on, as matters about which it is not expedient to trouble themselves,—they do not care one way or the other, but find it the easier and more respectable plan to admit the truth of the gospel, and think no more about it. Such a vain complimentary belief is rather an insult to our holy faith than a thing to be rejoiced in. But, dear friends, we want more than this faith of indifference, which is little more than dishonest unbelief ; we want men to believe for themselves, because they are personally convinced and have felt in themselves the saving power of Christ Jesus. We pray that nominal believers may treat the doctrines of revelation, not as dogmas, but as facts ; not as opinions, but as verities ; as surely facts as the events of history, as much verities as the actual incidents of every day life ; for, alas, the grand doctrines of eternal truth are frequently treated as venerable nonentities, and have no effect whatever upon the conduct of those who profess to receive them, because they do not realise them as matters of fact, or see their solemn bearings. It is shocking to reflect that a change in the weather has more effect on some men's lives than the dread alternative of heaven or hell. A woman's glance affects them more than the eye of God. We, therefore, desire to see men really and truly believing the facts of the gospel, in an honest, practical manner.

We cannot, however, be content with this; we labour *that those around us may savingly believe by putting their trust in the Lord Jesus Christ.* This is the grand saving act : the man brings his soul and commits it to Christ for safe keeping, and that entrusting of the soul to Jesus saves him. He makes the Saviour trustee of his spiritual estates, and leaves himself and all his eternal interests in those dear hands which once were nailed to the cross. Oh, how we long to see the Holy Spirit bringing men to this, that they may believe in Jesus Christ by resting in him and trusting upon him. For this we live, for this we would be content to die, that many might believe.

The end we aim at is that men may so believe in Jesus that they may be altogether changed in their relation towards God, for "many believed *and turned unto the Lord.*" What does that mean ? It means that these heathen gave up their idols and began to worship the only living and true God. We desire, dear hearers, that faith in the Lord Jesus may lead you to give up the objects of your idolatrous love, yourselves, your money, your pleasures, the world, the flesh, the devil ; for there be some whose God is their belly, and who glory in their shame. When a man believes in Jesus Christ he puts away his false gods, and worships the great Father of spirits ; he makes no inferior object the aim of his being, but henceforth lives for the glory of God. This is a glorious turning, a complete conversion of the man's heart and soul.

To turn to God means not merely to forsake the false god for the true, but to turn from the love of sin. Sin lies that way, but God's glory lies in the opposite quarter. He who looks sinward has his back to God—he who looks Godward has his back to sin. It is blessed conversion when men turn from the folly of sin to the glory of God. With weeping and supplication do men so turn, confessing their wrong-doing, lamenting their transgressions, abhorring their evil lustings, desiring pardon, and hoping for renewal of their nature. Precious in the sight of the Lord are the tears of penitence and the sighs of contrite hearts. We can never be satisfied with the results of our ministry unless faith leads man to hearty repentance towards God, an intense loathing of their sins, and an actual forsaking of them.

To turn to God means that henceforth God shall be sought in prayer. " Behold he prayeth " is one of the indications of a true convert. The man who lives without prayer lives without God, but the man who has turned to God is familiar with the mercy-seat. What a turning it is when the eye is turned upward to seek the Lord with the solemn glancing of the eye, when none but God is near. To turn to God means to yield yourself obediently to his sway, to be willing to do what he bids, to think what he teaches, and to be what he commands. Faith is nothing unless it brings with it a willing and obedient mind. Wilful rebellion is the child of unbelief, sincere obedience is the offspring of humble believing. "They believed, and turned unto the Lord." We want men, indeed, so to turn that their whole life shall be a going towards God, a growing more like him, a closer communing with him, leading on to the soul's becoming perfectly like him, and dwelling for ever where he is.

Now, dear friends, when I speak thus of believing and turning unto God some will say, " Well, but that must be a very easy matter, only to believe and turn." Yes, my brethren, it appears simple, but it is none the less vitally essential. " He that believeth on the Lord Jesus hath everlasting life ; but he that believeth not is condemned already, because he hath not believed." You say, " Why make all this stir about it?" Just because upon this apparently little matter depends the present and eternal condition of the sinner. To believe and to turn to God is to be delivered from the present dominion of sin, and from the future punishment of it: to be without faith and without God is to be without joy here and without hope hereafter. Brothers and sisters in Christ, this is what you and I must aim at in all our attempts to influence our fellow men. It may be useful to reform them; but it is far better that grace should regenerate them. God speed every effort to promote sobriety, chastity, thrift, honesty, and morality ; but you and I are sent for something more than this, our work goes deeper and is more difficult ; it is not ours to wash the blackamoor, but to seek to change his skin ; we do not so much pray that the lion may be tamed as that he may be turned into a lamb. It may be well to lop the branches of the tree of sin, but our business is to lay the axe at the root of the trees by leading men to turn to God. This is a change, not of the outward conduct merely, but of the heart ; and if we do not see this result, if men do not believe and turn to God, we have laboured in vain, and spent our strength for naught and in vain. If there are no believings and turnings to the Lord, we may get us to our secret chambers and bewail ourselves before God because none have believed our report, and the arm of the Lord has not been revealed. There is the object—aim at it, saying, " This one thing I do." Praying in the Holy Ghost, and depending upon his power, push on with this one sole object. Drive at it, you teachers in the Sabbath-school ; do not be satisfied with instructing the children, labour to have them converted. Drive at it, you preachers ; do not believe that you have done your work when you have taught the people, you must never rest till they believe in Jesus Christ. Pursue this end in every sermon or Sabbath-school address; throw your whole soul into this one object. Yours must not be a cold inculcation of an external morality, but a warm enthusiasm for an inward regeneration. You are not to bring men to believe in themselves and so become self-made men, but to lead them to believe in Jesus, and to become new creatures in him. There is our end and aim, are we all alive to it ?

II. Secondly, let us consider THE POWER BY WHICH THIS CAN BE ATTAINED,—"The hand of the Lord was with them." None ever believe in Jesus except those in whom God's arm has been revealed, for Jesus says, " No man can come to me except the Father which hath sent me draw him." But, brethren, in answer to prayer that power has been revealed among his people, and is with them still. His arm is not shortened that he cannot save, neither has he withdrawn it from his church. Be encouraged while I suggest to you a few thoughts. The hand of God is upon many of our friends before we speak to them. It is most pleasant to me when I am seeing inquirers, to observe how God makes ready the hearts of my hearers. I am studying a certain subject, and praying to God for a blessing on it, and upstairs in a chamber, which I have never seen, one of my hearers is being made ready for my message ; he is smitten with a sense of sin, or troubled with uneasy thoughts, or rendered hopeful of better things, and thus he is being made ready to accept the Christ whom I shall preach to him ; yes, and ready to accept that particular form of the gospel message which the Spirit of God gave me when I preached. There on a sick bed will lie a woman painfully exercised with the sad memory of her sinful life, in order that when she comes up to the house of God every word may have power over her. Sickness and pain, shame and poverty, often produce a condition of mind most hopeful for the reception of the gospel. A man well to do in circumstances has been ruined in business, he despairs of happiness below, and therefore comes to hear the gospel, made willing to seek his happiness above. Another has lately felt failures of bodily strength, and so has been warned that life is frail, and thus he is prepared to listen to the admonitions which speak of eternity. Courage, minister of God : you are nothing, but the Almighty God is with you. When you lift your hand to build the house of the Lord, omnipotence works with you, and makes your labour a success. Every revolution of those awful wheels, so ponderous that even the prophet said, " O wheel !" is working to accomplish the object which is near your heart. The stars in their courses fight for you. The stones of the field are in league with you. Eternal wisdom plans for you, infinite power works with you, boundless patience perseveres with you, and almighty love will conquer by you. " The hand of the Lord was with them." What more do we want ? Sow, brother, for God has ploughed. Go up and build, for God has prepared the stones and made ready the foundation.

Moreover, the hand of the Lord is with his people in helping the teachers and preachers themselves. There are strange impulses which come over us at times, which make us think and say what otherwise had never crossed our minds, and these work with power upon men's minds. If you will live to win souls it shall be given you in the self-same hour what ye shall speak. You will often say to an inquirer what you would not have beforehand arranged to say, but God, who knows that inquirer's heart better than you do, has prevented your saying what you would have liked to have said, and has led you to say what you afterwards judged to be a mistake. My experience teaches me that we are often wise in our ignorance, and as often foolish in our wisdom. We have frequently done best when we felt that we did but badly. If we will but trust God and be whole-hearted in the winning of souls we shall have a power assisting us in our speech of which the greatest orator in the world is not aware. Speak in the House of Commons for a party, and you will have to look within for aid, but speak in the house of the Lord and you may look upward for spiritual aid. The poet invokes the fabled muses, but for you, O servant of the Lord, there is real help from a higher source. Think of this, ye workers, and be encouraged.

Besides providence and the gracious help by which good men speak, there is a distinct work of the Spirit of God upon the hearts of men where the gospel is preached. Not only is the Spirit in the Word, but over and above that, in his own elect God worketh most effectually, so the truth is rendered irresistible. Let us never forget where our great strength lieth, for in this matter we must rely alone upon the *Spirit* of God. How often has God wrought in the power of his grace by making men feel the majesty of the word. They come, perhaps, to hear the preacher out of the idlest curiosity, they look for something which shall amuse them; but the truth comes home to them and searches their heart. Simple as the language is, "as if an angel spake they hear the solemn sound"; it goes through them like a dart, and they cannot help feeling, "Surely God was there, and he spoke with me."

The Spirit of God makes men recollect their sins : they try to forget them, but sometimes they cannot; sad memories steal over them, and wholesome regrets thrill their very souls. Men who have been giddy and careless, and forgetful, have on a sudden found themselves turning over the pages of their old diaries, and with thoughtfulness reviewing the past : all this leads to repentance and faith. That same Spirit makes men see the beauty of holiness; they cannot help admiring it, though they are far from it. They are charmed with the loveliness of the character of Jesus, and begin to feel that there is something about it which they would wish to imitate. When the preacher proclaims the way of salvation the same Spirit leads men to admire it, and to say within themselves, "There is something here which human wisdom could never have devised," and they begin to long for a share in it. A wish takes possession of their heart, as though some strange bird from an unknown land had flown into their souls, and had amazed them with a new song. They do not know where the desire came from, but they feel strangely bound to entertain the stranger. Sometimes also the Spirit blows like a hurricane through men's hearts, and they have been borne along by its power without the will to resist. As when a tempest rushes across the sea, and drives the frail bark before it helplessly, so have I known the divine Spirit sweep away the peace and quiet of the soul's self-righteousness, stir up the deeps of inward trouble, make the soul reel to and fro and stagger like a drunken man, and impel the heart forward to the iron-bound coast of self-despair, where every false hope and vain-glorious trust has been wrecked for ever. Glory be to God when this is the case, for then the soul is driven to cling to Jesus.

Yes, brethren, it is not the preacher, and it is not altogether what the preacher says, but there is a power abroad, as potent as that by which the worlds were made. Unbelievers sometimes ask, "Where is your God?" O sirs, if you once felt the power of the great Spirit you would never ask that question. "Since the fathers fell asleep," say they, "all things continue as they were;" but this they willingly are ignorant of, that new creations are being wrought every day, that there are men and women alive in this world who are neither liars nor enthusiasts, who can declare that upon their spirit the eternal power and Godhead has operated and changed them, conquering them, and holding them henceforth as willing captives to its supreme majesty. Yes, brethren, there is a hand of the Lord, and that hand of the Lord is with his people still. If it be not, then we shall see no believing and no turning to God; but since it is still at work among us, let us work on, for as surely as we live we shall see great numbers converted to God, and God will be glorified.

III. Let us now dwell upon THE DESIRABLENESS OF CONVERSIONS. It is no new thing to you and to me to see many believing and turning to God. These two-and-twenty years God's hand has been stretched out still : we have had no spasm of revival, we have not alternated between furious spurts and sudden lulls, but month by month, I think I might say Sabbath by Sabbath, souls have been saved, and the church has grown exceedingly, and God has been glorified. What we have enjoyed we desire to retain—yea, we would have more. The Lord says to us what he said to the church at Philadelphia, "Hold fast what thou hast, that no man take thy crown," and our crown is the crown of soul winning, which we must hold fast, for we cannot endure to lose it. This must be our crown, that we have preached the gospel, both minister and church members, and have been all of us soul-winners. We desire this because, first of all, we desire to see truth, godliness, virtue, and holiness extended. Who among you does not ? Does not every good man wish others to be good, every honest man wish others to be honest ? Does not every man who loves his family desire that other families should be well-ordered ? Oh, then, if there were no nobler reason, you may desire that men may be converted, since conversion is the root of everything that is pure, and lovely, and of good report.

You desire, too, that your fellow-creatures should be happy, but there is no such happiness as that which springs out of reconciliation to God. The peace which you yourselves enjoy through pardoned sin must surely make you desire that others may possess the same. If religion be indeed a source of perennial joy to yourself, you are inhuman if you do not wish others to drink of it. Brother, as you would make eyes sparkle, as you would make countenances radiant with delight, as I know you would spread gladness on all sides, desire above all things that your children, your relations, your neighbours, your friends, should be converted to God. Thus shall thorns and briars give place to myrtles and rose, and deserts shall be turned into gardens of the Lord.

You also desire conversion, I am sure, because you feel the dreadful hazard of unconverted men. You have not yet subscribed to the modern doctrine that these men and women around you are only two-legged cats and dogs and horses, and will ultimately die out and cease to be. You believe in the God-given immortality of human souls, a heritage from which no man can escape, the noblest of all man's endowments ; in itself the highest of all boons, though sin may pervert it into the direst of all necessities. You would have scant motives for desiring men's conversion if you did not believe that there is another and everlasting state ; but, believing that men live hereafter, and exist for ever, you must, I am sure, be eager that men may escape from the wrath to come. Knowing the terrors of the Lord, you would persuade men; judging that there is one of two things for them all, either " These shall go away into everlasting punishment"; or else, "The righteous into life eternal," you can never rest until you feel convinced that those about you are partakers of life eternal. Look at any unconverted person, and your sympathies should be aroused. If I saw tokens of fever, or marks of consumption in the face of any one I loved, I should be struck with alarm; what, then, must I feel when I see damnation—as I do see it—in the face of every unbeliever? How is it that we are not more distressed than we are when men are perishing in their sins? Why, my brethren, are we not more intent upon the conversion of men? Let these questions humble us and cause great searchings of heart. It is a shame to us that we have so little of the mind of Christ, so little compassion for men's souls.

Moreover, brethren, self-preservation is a law of nature, and the Church can never preserve herself except by increasing from the world by conversion. Where are the preachers for the next generation? To-day they are amongst the ungodly, and we must labour to bring them to God. Where are the stones that are to make the next course in the walls of our Zion? They are unquarried yet, and we must, by God's grace, excavate them. We who now labour for the Lord will soon go our ways. Our thrones and crowns are waiting for us, and the angels are beckoning us away; who will fill our places? Who will bear the banner? Who will blow the trumpet? Who will wield the sword? We must find new champions in the ranks of the foe; they must be born unto God, and we must pray that this may be accomplished by our instrumentality.

Seek conversions *for Christ's sake.* You know the agony and bloody sweat; shall these be spent in vain? You know the nailing to the cross and the shriek of "Why hast thou forsaken me?" shall these be unrewarded? You have thought over and trusted in the bitter pangs of your Redeemer's death; shall he not see of the travail of his soul? Shall he not be satisfied? These lost sheep are *his* sheep, for whom he shed his precious blood; these lost pieces of money are *his* money, and they bear his image and superscription; shall they not be found? These lost sons, away there spending their living in riotousness, are *his* brothers, children of *his* Father; do you not desire for Jesus' sake that they should be brought home?

Dear friends, what joy it will be to yourselves if men believe and turn to the Lord by your means. I put that motive last, and hope it will not be the strongest, but it may yet be one of the liveliest. What joy it will be to yourselves if you see many converted! Somebody has asked, "If the heathen are not evangelised, what will become of them?" I will put another question of a far more practical character. If you do not try to evangelise the heathen, *what will become of you?* Do not so much inquire about *their* destiny as your own, if you have no care for their salvation. He who never seeks the conversion of another is in imminent danger of being damned himself. I do not believe in any man's salvation who is wrapped up in self, assuredly he is not saved from selfishness. I cannot believe in any man's possessing the Spirit of God who is indifferent to the condition of others, for one of the first fruits of the Spirit is love. Even as flowers at their very first bloom-ing shed their perfume, so do the saved ones in their earliest days of grace desire the good of their fellows. I know that one of my earliest impulses when I first looked to Christ and lost the burden of my sin was to tell everybody around me of the blessings I had received, for I longed to make others as happy as I was. I do fear me that you who never try to win souls lack an essential part of the Christian character. I leave the question with your own consciences.

IV. Fourthly, let us enquire, WHAT WE CAN DO TO PROMOTE CONVERSIONS. Conversion is God's work: it cannot be wrought without his hand. Without him we can do nothing. Our hand is far too puny for such a work; the power of the first disciples and our own lies in the fact mentioned in the text,—"The hand of the Lord was with them." Still, there are certain circumstances under which that hand will work, and there are hindrances which will restrain it. Let us think awhile. First, then, if sinners are to be converted *we must distinctly aim at it.* As a rule, a man does what he tries to do, and not that which is mere by-play. The conversion of sinners is not one of those things which a man is likely to accomplish without intending it. Sometimes in the sovereignty of God a preacher who does not aim at conversion may nevertheless be made useful, for God works as he wills; but largely, and as a rule men do not win souls if they do not eagerly desire to do so. Fishing for men cannot be carried out by throwing in the net anyhow, without caring whether fish be caught or no. Few traders become rich by accident, they generally have to plod and work hard for money: and to be rich in treasures of saved souls you must aim at it and labour for it. I am struck with astonishment as I think how many sermons are preached, how many Sunday-school addresses are given, how many religious books are written of which you are quite sure that the intention was not immediate conversion. It is thought that in some unknown way these good things may accidentally contribute to men's salvation, but they are not aimed at as their present object. Ah, brother, if you want men to come to Christ you must preach Christ to them with all your heart, with this design, that immediately they may close in with Christ, and at once give their hearts to Jesus. Yes, and you are to pray that they may do so through the present effort which you are making for their good. There is the target, and if you continue to shoot into the air long enough an arrow may perhaps strike it; but, man alive, if you want to win the prize of archery you had better fix your eye upon the white and take your aim distinctly and with skill. If an individual would win souls he must bend his whole soul to it and make it the object of his whole energy.

Next to that we must take care if we would have souls won that we *press upon them the truths which God usually blesses.* Shall I read to you the verse before my text? Here it is: "They spake unto the Grecians, preaching the Lord Jesus, and the hand of the Lord was with them." Now, if we do not preach Jesus Christ we shall not see souls saved. There are certain forms of doctrines which condemn themselves by working out their own extinction. Did you ever hear of a minister whose preaching leaned towards Unitarianism but what the congregation sooner or later began to diminish? Though many such preachers have been men of great ability, they have not as a rule been able to keep the dead thing on its feet. You shall go into our small towns, and you may find an ancient chapel which was once an Independent, or a Presbyterian, or it may be a Baptist chapel ; but if you see over the door " *Unitarian*," you have, as a rule, seen all that there is. There is neither church nor congregation worthy of the name ; frequently the place is never opened at all, and the grass grows knee deep on the path to the door. Even when these little places are used, you will generally find that they contain half a dozen nobodies who think themselves everybody as to intellect and culture. It is a religion of the utmost value to spiders, for those insects are able to spin their webs in the meeting-houses without fear. Who ever heard, who ever will hear of a Unitarian Whitfield, or a Socinian Moody gathering twenty thousand people to listen to a Christless gospel ? It is a phenomenon which never has been seen and never will be. Men's instincts lead them to turn away from a creed which contains so little which can solace the troubled soul.

If we want souls saved we must equally avoid the modern intellectual system in all its phases. " Oh," cries somebody, " you should hear the great Mr. Bombast. It is—Oh, I cannot tell you what it is, but something very wonderful ; it is an intellectual treat." Just so ; but how many conversions are wrought by this wonderful display of genius ? How many hearts are broken by fine rhetoric ? How many broken hearts are healed by philosophy ? So far as I have observed, I find that God does not save souls by intellectual treats.

Certain views as to man's future are equally to be kept clear of, if you would be the means of conversion. Diminish your ideas of the wrath of God and the terrors of hell, and in that proportion you will diminish the results of your work. I could not conceive a Bunyan or a Baxter, or any other great soul-winner, falling into these new notions, or if he did there would be an end to his success. Other crotchets and novelties of doctrine are also to be let alone, for they are not likely to promote your object, but will most probably divert men's attention from the vital point. Dear brothers and sisters, if you want a harvest, look well to your seed. Time was when gardeners threw all the little potatoes on one side for seed, and then they had bad crops ; but now I have seen them pick out the very best and put them by. " We must have good seed," say they. If I had to sow my fields with wheat I would not take the tail corn. I should grudge no expense about seed, for it would be false economy to buy any but the very best. Go preach, teach, and instruct with the best doctrine, even that of God's word ; for depend upon it though the result is not in your hands, yet it very much depends upon what you teach. O, eternal and ever blessed Spirit, guide thy servants into all truth !

Next to this, if you want to win souls for Christ, *feel a solemn alarm about them.* You cannot make them feel if you do not feel yourself. Believe their danger, believe their helplessness, believe that only Christ can save them, and talk to them as if you meant it. The Holy Spirit will move them by first moving *you.* If you can rest without their being saved *they* will rest too ; but if you are filled with an agony for them, if you cannot bear that they should be lost, you will soon find that they are uneasy too. I hope you will get into such a state that you will dream about your child, or about your hearer perishing for lack of Christ, and start up at once and begin to cry, " O God, give me converts or I die." Then you will have converts ; there is no fear about that. God does not send travail pangs to his servants without causing them to abound in spiritual children. There will be new births to God when you are agonising for them.

But, let me add, *there must be much prayer.* I delignt to be at prayer-meetings where the brethren will not let the Lord go except he bless them, when a brother prays, choking as he speaks, tears rolling down his cheeks as he pleads with God to have mercy on the sons of men. I am always certain that sinners are ordained to be blessed when I see saints thus compelled to plead with God for them. In your closets alone, at your family altars, and in your gatherings for prayer be importunate, and the hand of the Lord must and will be with you. Cry aloud and spare not, plead as for your lives, and bring forth your strong arguments, for only by prevailing with God will you be enabled to prevail with men.

Then there must be added to prayer *direct personal effort on the part of all of you.* Great numbers may be saved by my preaching if the Holy Spirit blesses it, but I shall expect larger numbers if you all turn preachers, if every brother and sister here becomes a witness for Christ. Are you indolent ? Are any of you beginning to sleep ? I charge you, wake up. By the love you bear to Jesus, and by the love you bear to your fellow men, begin at once to seek the conversion of those who dwell around you. O my beloved, do not become lukewarm. My heart fails me at the very thought. If you are earnest, I live ; if you grow slothful, my spirit dies within me.

Last of all, if you want to see many converts, *expect them.* " According-ing to your faith so be it unto you." Look out for them ; believe that God will bless every sermon, and go a-hunting after the sermon to see where the converts are. As a company of sutlers and camp-followers generally follow every army, and after a battle go up to strip the slain, so if you cannot preach I would have you follow after the warriors to gather in the spoil. No one needed to urge the voracious spoilers to prowl over the field of Sedan or Gravelotte, but now it even seems needful to persuade you to collect a far nobler prey. Come ye up, come ye up, ye servants of the Lord, and divide the spoil with the strong. Christ has fought your battle, his arrows have been sharp in the hearts of the King's enemies, the two-edged sword has smitten right and left; come ye up, ye sons of Jacob, to the prey, and gather in the converts as your spoil. Speak with the young converts, cheer the broken hearts, comfort the seekers, and bring into his palace trophies for your Lord. Verily, I say unto you, if ye look not for conversions neither shall ye obtain them, but then blame not the Lord ; ye are not straitened in him, but in your own bowels. God bless you, beloved, and may we have a larger increase to this church during the next month than we have had for years past, that our God may have greater praise.

Conversions Encouraged

"But if from thence thou shalt seek the Lord thy God, thou shalt find him, if thou seek him with all thy heart and with all thy soul. When thou art in tribulation, and all these things are come upon thee, even in the latter days, if thou turn to the Lord thy God, and shalt be obedient unto his voice; (for the Lord thy God is a merciful God;) he will not forsake thee, neither destroy thee, nor forget the covenant of thy fathers which he sware unto them."—Deuteronomy iv. 29 — 31.

LAST Sabbath-day the title of my discourse was "Conversions desired," and my earnest prayer to God has been that the effect of this morning's sermon may be conversions accomplished. I cannot be happy unless I indulge the hope that some will this morning turn unto God with full purpose of heart, led to do so by the power of divine grace. For this I sought the Lord, and at this I resolved to aim. I asked myself, "What is the most likely subject in the hand of the Holy Spirit to lead men to the Lord? Shall I preach the terrors of the Lord, or shall I proclaim the sweetness of divine mercy? Each of these has its proper use, but which will be most likely to answer our design to-day?" I remembered the fable of the sun and the wind. These rival powers competed as to which could compel the traveller to cast away his cloak. The wind blew boisterously, and tugged at the garment as if it would tear it from the traveller's shoulders, but he buttoned it the closer about him, and held it firmly with his hand. The battle was not to the strong and threatening. Then the sun burst forth from behind a cloud, when the wind had ceased its blustering, and smiled upon the traveller with warmth of kindness until he loosened his cloak, and by-and-by was glad to take it off altogether: the soft, sweet influence of the sun had vanquished where the storm had raged in vain. So I thought, perhaps if I preach the tender mercy of God, and his readiness to forgive, it may be to my hearers as the warm beams of the sun to the traveller, and they will cast away the garments of their sin and self-righteousness. I know that the arrows of love are keen, and wound many hearts which are invulnerable to the sword of wrath. O that these sacred darts may win the victory this day! When ships at sea apprehend a storm they will gladly make for an open harbour, but if it be doubtful whether they can enter the port they will rather weather the tempest than run the risk of being unable to enter the harbour's mouth. Some havens can only be entered when the tide happens to be at the flood, and therefore the captain will not venture: but when the welcome signals are flying and it is clear that there is plenty of water, and that they may safely run behind the breakwater, they hesitate no longer, but make sail for the shelter. Let seeking souls know this day that the Lord's harbour of refuge is open, the port of free grace can be reached, that there is sea room for the hugest transgressor, and love enough to float the greatest sinner into port. Ho, weather-beaten vessels, ye may come and welcome! There is no need that even for a solitary hour ye should run the risk of the tempest of almighty wrath; you are invited to find shelter and to enjoy it now.

It is rather singular that having these ideas floating in my mind, and desiring to preach free grace and abounding mercy, I should have found my text in Deuteronomy. Why, that is a book of the law, and is plentifully besprinkled with terrible threatenings, and yet I find a gospel theme in it: yea, and one of the very richest! As I read it I admired it for its connection as well as for its own fulness, it seems to me so pleasant to find this lily among thorns. As in the wintry months of the opening year one finds a crocus smiling up from the cold soil and in its golden cup offering a taste of the sunlight which summer will more fully bring, so amid the ungenial pages of the law I see this precious gospel declaration, which like the spring flower assures us that God's love is yet alive, and will bring us happier times. My thoughts also likened this passage to the water which leaped from the smitten rock, for the law is like a rock, and the Pentateuch is hard and stern as granite; but here in its very bowels we find a crystal spring of which the thirsty may drink. I likened the text also to the manna lying on the desert sand, the bread of heaven glittering like a shining pearl upon the barren soil of the wilderness. Here amid the fiery statutes of the law, and the terrible judgments threatened by the God of Sinai you see this manna of mercy dropped about your tents this morning, as fresh, I hope, to you as if but newly fallen. May you eat of it and live for ever.

Let us come to our text at once. The Lord here encourages sinners to turn to himself, and find abundant grace. He encourages sinners who had violated his plainest commandments, who had made idols, and so had corrupted themselves, and had consequently been visited with captivity, and other chastisements—he invites them to turn from their evil ways and seek his face. I feel moved to say at the commencement of this discourse that if the text has any limited aspect, if it is to be regarded as uttered to any special character among transgressors, it peculiarly belongs to *backsliders;* for the people to whom it was first addressed were the people of God, but they had set up idols, and so had wandered; and it is to them chiefly, though not to them exclusively, that these encouragements to repentance are presented. As probably there are some backsliders here who once stood in the church of God, but have been cut off therefrom, who once were very zealous and earnest in the cause of God, but have now become utterly indifferent to all religion,

I charge such to take this text home to themselves. Take every syllable of it into your own heart, backslider. Read, mark, learn, and inwardly digest the same, and may the text bring you to your knees and to your God. It gives you a pointed invitation to return from your wanderings and end your weary backslidings by coming once more to your Father's house, for he will not forsake you, nor destroy you, nor forget the covenant of mercy which he has made on your behalf. Happy are you that you may return ; happy shall I be if you do return. I thought I would lay special stress upon this, because the Lord himself, and his ministers with him, rejoice more over one lost sheep that returns to the Shepherd of souls than over ninety and nine that went not astray. There is rejoicing when a man finds a treasure which he never had before, but it is scarcely equal to the joy of the woman who found the piece of money which was hers already, but which she had lost. Glad is the house when the babe is born, but deeper is the joy when the lost son is found. My soul longs to see the Lord bring home his banished ones, and to be the means of gathering his scattered ones.

Still, the text is fully applicable to all sinners—to all who have corrupted themselves and done evil in the sight of the Lord to provoke him to anger. The Ever-merciful encourages them to turn to him with full purpose of heart, by assuring them that he will not forsake them. There seems to me to be in the text three points which should induce an earnest seeking of his face at once, for here is, first, *a time mentioned;* secondly, *a way appointed;* and thirdly, *encouragement given.*

I. First, then, in the text there is A TIME MENTIONED. Look at it . "If from thence thou shalt seek the Lord. . . When thou art in tribulation, and all these things are come upon thee, even in the latter days."

The time in which the Lord bids you seek him, O you unforgiven ones, is first of all, "*from thence,*" that is, from the condition into which you have fallen, or the position which you now occupy. According to the connection of the text, the offending Israelites were supposed to be in captivity, scattered among various nations, dwelling where they were compelled to worship gods of wood and stone, which could not see, nor hear, nor feel, nor eat, nor smell ; yet "from thence"—from the unhallowed heathen villages, from their lone sorrows by the waters of Babylon, from their captivity in far-off Chaldea, they were bidden to turn unto the Lord and obey his voice. Their surroundings were not to be allowed to hinder their prayers. Perhaps, dear friend, at this time you are dwelling amongst ungodly relations ; if you begin to speak about religion you are put down at once, you hear nothing that can help you in the way to better things, but very much that would hinder you ; nevertheless, do not delay, but "from thence," even from thence seek you the Lord, for it is written : " If thou seek him he will be found of thee." It may be you are living in a neighbourhood where everything is hostile to the gospel of Jesus Christ, and injurious even to your morals. Time was, and you may remember it with regret, when you were a child upon the knee of a pious mother, when you spent your Sabbaths in the Sunday-school, when the Bible was read in your house every day : but now all these helps are taken from you, and everything around is dragging you down to greater and yet greater sin. Do not, however, make this a reason for delay ; as well might a man refuse to go to a physician because he lives in an unhealthy locality, or a drowning man refuse the life-boat because a raging sea surrounds him. Hasten rather than slacken your speed. Do not tarry till your position improve; do not wait till you move into a godly family, or live nearer to the means of grace, for if thou seek him "from thence" he will be found of thee.

But you will tell me that it is not so much your regret that others are ungodly among whom you dwell, but that you yourself are in a wretched condition of heart, for you have followed after one sin and another until evil has become a habit with you, and you cannot shake it off. Like a rolling thing before the whirlwind you are driven on; an awful force impels you from bad to worse. Arouse yourself, O man, for immediate action, for if you wait till you have conquered this evil force by your own strength, if you delay to turn unto God until you are free from the dominion of sin, then assuredly you will wait for ever, and perish in your folly. If you could vanquish evil by your own power you would not need to seek the Lord, for you would have found salvation in yourself; but be not so infatuated as to dream of such a thing. To-day, "from thence," from the place where you now are, turn your face to your Father who is in heaven, and seek him through Jesus Christ. Recollect that hymn which ought to be sung every Sabbath-day in our assemblies—

"Just as I am—and waiting not
To rid my soul of one dark blot,
To thee, whose blood can cleanse each spot,
O Lamb of God, I come."

Every verse begins with "Just as I am," and so must your prayer, your faith, your hope begin. The whole hymn commences "Just as I am," and so must your Christian life be started.

The Lord invites you as you are and where you are. Are you one of a godless family, the only one in the house who has felt any serious thought at all? Come, then, and tarry not, for the Lord invites you. Are you the one man in a large workshop, where all the rest are irreligious? Admire his sovereign grace, accept the call, and henceforth be the Lord's. The Lord invites those of you who have gone to the ends of the earth in sin, and brought yourselves into captivity by your rebellion. To-day, even to-day, he bids you seek him "with all your heart and with all your soul."

With regard to the time of turning, it is well worthy of our notice that we are specially encouraged to turn unto the Lord if we are in a painful plight. Our text says, "*When thou art in tribulation.*" Are you sick? Have you felt ill for some time? Does your weakness increase upon you? Are you apprehensive that this sickness may even be unto death? When thou art in such tribulation then thou mayest return to him. A sick body should lead us the more earnestly to seek healing for our sick soul. Are you poor, have you come down from a comfortable position to one of hard labour and of scant provision? When thou art in this tribulation then turn to the Lord, for he has sent thee this need to make thee see thy yet greater necessity, even thy need of himself. The empty purse should make thee remember thy soul poverty, the bare cupboard should lead thee to see the emptiness of all thy carnal confidences, and accumulating debts should compel thee to calculate how much thou owest to thy Lord. It is possible that your trials are very bitter at this moment, because you are expecting to lose some whom you dearly love, and this is like rending half yourself away. One dear child is hardly cold in the tomb, and your heart is bleeding when you think of this loss—and now another is sickening and will follow the first. When thou art in this tribulation, then be sure to seek the Lord, for his pitying heart is open to thee, and he will sanctify this grief to noblest purposes. Is it possible that I speak to one whose sins have become so open as to have been punished by the law of the land? Have you lost your character? Will none employ you any longer? When thou art in this tribulation then turn to thy Lord, for he will receive earth's castaways, and make criminals his sons. Have you suffered from the just verdict of society because you are vicious, dishonest, and disreputable? Are you at this time despised and looked down upon? Yet even to you would I say, when thou art in tribulation, when every door is shut, when all hands are held up against you, even then seek the Lord, and he will be found of you. If your father scarcely dares to think upon your name, if you have been a grief to your sister's heart, and have brought your mother's grey hairs with sorrow to the grave, yet now, even in this shameful estate, when thou art in tribulation turn to the Lord thy God.

Doubtless there are some people who will never be saved except they come into tribulation. Their substance must all be spent, and a mighty famine must come upon them, the citizens of the far country must refuse them aid, and with hungry bellies they must stand at the trough and be willing to feed with the swine, or else it will never occur to them to say, " I will arise and go to my father." No matter how deep your trouble, your safest and wisest course is to flee to God in Christ Jesus, and put your trust in him.

Notice further, when you feel that the judgments of God have begun to overtake you, then you may come to him : " When thou art in tribulation and *all these things*—these threatened things—*are come upon thee.*" There are many in this world who feel as if their sin had at last found them out, and had commenced to be a hell to them. The manslayer has overtaken them, and is striking at them with terrible blows. " Ah," says one, " my great sins have provoked at last God, and all men may see what he has done unto me, for he has removed my choicest mercies from me. I despised a father's instruction—that father is dead ; I did not value my mother's tears—my mother sleeps under the sod. The dear wife who used to beg me to walk to the house of God with her ; I slighted and treated her with unkindness, and death has removed her from my bosom. The little child that used to climb my knee and sing its little hymns, and persuade me to pray, has gone too! God has found me out at last, and begun to strip me. These are only the first drops of an awful shower of wrath from which I cannot escape. Alas, while one mercy after another is removed, my former joys have been embittered, and are joys no more. I go to the theatre as I used to do, but I do not enjoy it. I see beneath the paint and the gilt, and it seems a mockery of my woe. My old companions come to see me, and they would sing me the old songs, but I cannot bear them ; their mirth grates on my ear—at times it seems to be mere idiotic yelling. I used to get alone and philosophise and dote upon many things which afforded me comfort, but now I find no consolation in them—I have no joy of my thoughts now. The world is dreary, and my soul is weary. I am in the sere and yellow leaf, and all the world is fading with me. What little joy I had before has utterly departed, and no new joy comes. I am neither fit for God nor fit for the devil. I can find no peace in sin, and no rest in religion. Into the narrow way I fear I cannot enter, and in the broad way I am so jostled that I do not know how to pursue my course. Worst of all there is before me a dreadful outlook; I am filled with horrible apprehensions of the dread hereafter. I am afraid of the harvest which must follow the sad seed sowing of my misspent life. I have a dread of death upon me; I know not how near it may be, but it is too near, I know, and I am not prepared for it. I am overwhelmed with thoughts of the judgment to come. I hear the trump ringing in my ears when I am at my work. I hear the messengers of God's justice summoning me and saying, 'Come to judgment, come to judgment, come away.' A fearful sound is in mine ears, and I, whither shall I go?" Hear, O man, and be comforted, for now is the appointed time for thee to seek the Lord, for our text says, " When all these things are come upon thee, if thou turn unto the Lord thy God, he will not forsake thee neither destroy thee."

There is yet one more word which appears to me to contain great comfort in it, and it is this, " *even in the latter days.*" This expression may refer to the latter days of Jewish history, though I can scarcely think it does, because the Jews are not now guilty of idolatry. I rather think it must refer to the latter days of any one of their captivities and in our case to the latter days of life. Looking around me I see that many of you are advanced in years, and if you are unconverted I thank God I am as free to preach Christ to you as if you had been children or young men. If you have spent sixty or seventy years in rebellion against your God, you may return "even in the latter days." If your day is almost over, and you have arrived at the eleventh hour, when the sun touches the horizon, and evening shadows thicken, still he may call you into his vineyard and at the close of the day give you your penny. He is longsuffering and full of mercy, not willing that any should perish, and therefore he sends me out as his messenger to assure you that if you seek him he will be found of you, "even in the latter days." It is a beautiful sight, though it is mingled with much sadness, to see a very old man become a babe in Christ. It is sweet to see him, after he has been so many years the proud, wayward, self-confident master of himself, at last learning wisdom, and sitting at Jesus' feet. They hang up in the cathedrals and public halls old banners which have long been carried by the enemy into the thick of the fight. If they have been torn by shot and shell, so much the more do the captors value them: the older the standard the more honour is it, it seems, to seize it as a trophy. Men boast when they have carried off—

> " The flag that braved a thousand years
> The battle and the breeze."

Oh, how I wish that my Lord and Master would lay hold on some of you worn-out sinners, you who have been set up by the devil as standards of sin. O that the Prince of the kings of the earth would compel you to say, "Love conquers even me."

I will not leave this head till I have said that it gives me great joy to be allowed to preach an immediate gospel to you—a gospel which bids you turn unto God and find present salvation. Suppose for a moment that the gospel ran thus,—" You, sinner, shall be saved in twelve months time if you turn to God." Oh, sirs, I should count the days for you till the twelve months were gone. If it were written, "I will be found of you in March, 1877," I should weary over you till the auspicious season arrived, and say, "Mayhap they will die before mercy's hour has struck; spare them, good Lord." Yes, and if it were true that God would not hear you until next Sabbath-day I should like to lock you up and keep you out of harm's way, if I could, till that time arrived, lest you should die before the promised hour. If there were any way of insuring your lives, though you had to give all that you have for your soul, you might be glad to insure your life till next Lord's-day. But, blessed be God, the promise does not tarry; it is NOW! "To-day if ye will hear his voice." The gospel does not even bid you wait till you reach your home, or get to your bedside, but here and now, in that pew and at this moment, if you seek him with all your heart, and with all your soul, the Lord Jesus will be found of you, and present salvation shall be immediately enjoyed. Is it not encouraging to think that *just now* the Lord is waiting to be gracious.

II. But now, secondly, let us look at THE WAY APPOINTED. To find mercy, what are we bidden to do? "If from thence thou shalt seek the Lord thy God." We have not, then, to bring anything to God, but to seek *him*. We have not to seek a righteousness to bring to him, nor seek a state of heart which will fit us for him, but to seek *him* at once. Sinner, you have offended God, none but God can forgive you, for the offences are against himself. Seek him, then, that he may forgive you. It is essential that you seek him as a real existence, and a true person, believing that he is, and that he is a rewarder of them that diligently seek him. It is all in vain to seek sacraments, you must seek *him:* it is idle to go through forms of prayer, or to utter customary phrases of devotion, you must seek *him.* Your salvation lies in God, sinner, and your seeking must be after God. Do you understand this? It is not going to your priest or to your clergyman, or to your Bible or to your Prayer-book, or even to your knees in formal prayer ; but you must draw near to God in Christ Jesus, and he must be found of you as a man finds a treasure and takes it to be his own. "But where shall I find him?" saith one. When they sought God of old they went to the mercy-seat, for there the Lord had promised to speak with them. Now, the Lord Jesus Christ is that mercy-seat, sprinkled with precious blood, and if you want to find God, you must seek him in the person of Jesus Christ. Is it not written : "No man cometh unto the Father but by me !" Jesus is the one Mediator between God and man, and if you would find God, you must find him in the person of Jesus the Nazarene, who is also the Son of the Highest. You will find Jesus by believing him, trusting him, resting upon him. When you have trusted Jesus, you have found God in Jesus, for he hath said, "He that hath seen me, hath seen the Father." Then have you come to God when you have believed in Jesus

Christ. How simple this is ! How unencumbered with subtleties and difficulties ! When God gives grace, how easy and how plain is believing. Salvation is not by doing, nor by being, nor by feeling, but simply by believing. We are not to be content with self, but to seek the Lord. Being nothing in ourselves, we are to go out of ourselves to him. Being ourselves unworthy, we are to find worthiness in Jesus.

We are also to grasp the Lord as ours, for the text says, "Thou shalt seek the Lord *thy God.*" Sinners, that is a part of saving faith, to take God to be your God ; if he is only another man's God, he cannot save you ; he must be yours, yours, assuredly yours, yours to trust and love and serve all your days, or you will be lost.

Now, mark God's directions : "If thou seek him *with all thy heart and with all thy soul.*" There must be no pretence about this seeking. If you desire to be saved, there must be no playing and toying, trifling and feigning. The search must be real, sincere, and earnest, fervent, intense, thorough-going, or it will be a failure. Is this too much to ask ? Surely if anything in the world deserves earnestness it is this. If anything ought to arouse all a man's powers to energy, it is the salvation of his soul. You cannot win gold and attain riches without being in earnest in the pursuit : but what earnestness does this deserve *?* This obtaining eternal life, deliverance from eternal death, acceptance in the beloved, endless bliss ? Oh, men, if you sleep over anything, at any rate be awake here ! If you trifle upon any matters of importance, yet here at any rate be serious, solemn, and earnest. Here there must be no idling and no delay. Note that there is a repetition in the text. "If thou seek him *with all thy heart* and *with all thy soul,*" we must be doubly in earnest, heart and soul must be in the pursuit. Half-hearted seeking is no seeking at all. To ask for mercy from God and at the same time to be willing to be without it is a mere pretence of asking. If you are content to be put off with an inferior blessing, you are not seeking the Lord at all. I remember one who is now a member of this church who in a desperate fit of soul anxiety said solemnly to one of us, "I will never go to work again, I will neither eat nor drink till I have found the Saviour," and with that solemn resolve it was not long before he had found him. Oh, sirs, suppose you should be lost. Suppose you should perish while I am speaking ! I know of no reason why your pulse should continue to beat, or your breath should remain in your nostrils, and if at this moment you were to die, at that selfsame instant you would plunge amidst the flames of hell. Escape then at once. Even now make soul matters your sole concern. Whatever else you have to attend to, leave it alone, and attend first to this chief thing, the salvation of your soul. If a man were in a sinking vessel, he may have been a student of the classics, but he will not think of his stopping to translate an ode of Horace : he may have been a mathematician, but he will not sit down to work out an equation ; he will leap at once from the sinking vessel into the boat, for his object will be to save his life. And should it not be so as to our eternal life ? My soul, my soul, this must be saved, and with all my heart will I seek to God in Jesus Christ that I may find salvation.

The text further adds that we are to turn to him. Did you notice the thirtieth verse—"*If thou turn to the Lord thy God.*" It must be a thorough turn. You are looking now towards the world—you must turn in the opposite direction, and look Godward. It must not be an apparent turn, but a real change of the nature, a turning of the entire soul; a turning with repentance for the past, with confidence in Christ for the present, and with holy desires for the future. Heart, soul, life, speech, action, all must be changed. Except ye be converted ye cannot enter the kingdom of heaven. May God grant you such a turn as this, and to this end do you pray, "Turn me, and I shall be turned."

Then it is added, "*and be obedient to his voice*," for we cannot be saved in disobedience : Christ is not come to save his people in their sins, but from their sins. "If ye be willing and obedient, ye shall eat the good of the land : but if ye refuse and rebel, ye shall be devoured with the sword." Do you see, my dear unconverted hearers, what God's advice is to you ? It is that now you obey his gospel, and bow before the sceptre of his Son Jesus. He would have you own that you have erred, and entreat to be kept from erring again. Your proud self-will must yield, and your self-confidence must be renounced, and you must incline your ear and come unto him, "Hear and your soul shall live." This his Holy Spirit will grant you grace to do. This is the least that could be asked of you ; you could not expect the great King to pardon rebels and allow them to continue in rebellion : he could not allow you to continue in sin and yet partake of his grace. You know that such a course would not be worthy of a holy God.

Do you feel inclined at this moment to turn to the Lord ? Does some gentle power, you have never felt before, draw you beyond yourself ? Do you perceive that it would be well for you to be reconciled to your God and Father ? Do you feel some kindlings of regret, some sparks of good desire ? Then yield to the impulse : I trust it is the Holy Spirit within, working in you to will and to do of his own good pleasure. Yield at once : completely yield, and he will lead you by a way you know not, and bring you to Jesus, and in him shall find peace and rest, holiness, happiness, and heaven. Let this be the happy day. Bend before the Spirit's breath as the reed bows in the wind. Quench not the Spirit, grieve him no more—

" Lest slighted once the season fair
Should ne'er return again."

Beware lest bleeding love should never woo again, lest pitying grace should never more entreat, and tender mercy should never more cast its cords around you. The spouse said, " Draw me, we will run after thee," do you say the same. Behold, before you there is an open door, and within that door a waiting Saviour, will you perish on the threshold ?

III. Thirdly, the text contains VERY RICH ENCOURAGEMENTS. How does it run ? "For the Lord thy God is a merciful God ; *he will not forsake thee*." Catch at that sinner, "He will not forsake thee." If he were to say, "Let him alone, Ephraim is given unto idols," it would be all over with you ; but if you seek him he will not say, " Let him alone," nor take his Holy Spirit from you. You are not yet given up, I hope, or you would not have been here this morning to hear this sermon.

I thought when I woke this morning, and saw the snow and pitiless sleet driven by a vehement wind, that it was a pity I had studied such a subject, for I would like to have the house crowded with sinners, and they are not so likely to come out in bad weather. Just then I recollected that it was upon just such a morning as this that I found the Saviour myself, and that thought gave me much courage in coming here. I thought the congregation cannot be smaller than that of which I made one on that happy day when I looked to Christ. I believe that many will this morning be bought out and saved, for the Lord has not forsaken this congregation. I used to think he had given me up, and would not show me mercy after so long seeking in vain ; but he had not forsaken *me*, nor has he cast *you* off, O sinner ! If you seek him with all your heart, you may rest assured he will not forsake you.

And then it is added, " *Neither destroy thee.*" You have been afraid he would ; you have often thought the earth would open and swallow you ; you have been afraid to fall asleep lest you should never wake again ; but the Lord will not destroy you ; nay rather he will reveal his saving power in you.

There is a sweeter word still in the 29th verse : " *Thou shalt find him if thou seek him.*" I wish I could sing, and could extemporize a bit of music, for then I would stand here and sing those words : " Thou shalt find him if thou seek him." At any rate, the words have sweet melody in them to my ear and heart—" Thou shalt find him if thou seek him." I should like to whisper that sentence softly to the sick, and to shout it to the busy. It ought to linger long in your memories, and abide in your hearts—" Thou shalt find him if thou seek him." What more, poor sinner, what more dost thou want ?

Then there are two reasons given : " *For the Lord thy God is a merciful God.*" Oh, guilty soul, the Lord does not want to damn you, he does not desire to destroy you. Judgment is his strange work. Have you ever had to chasten your child ? When you have felt bound to punish severely by reason of a great fault, has it not been very hard work ? You have said to yourself a hundred times over, " What shall I do ? What shall I do to escape from the misery of causing pain to my dear child ? " You have been driven to chasten him or you would not have done it. God never sends a sinner to hell till justice demands it. He finds no joy in punishing. He swears, " As I live, saith the Lord, I have no pleasure in the death of him that dieth." Look at the judge when he puts on the black cap, does he do so with pleasure ? Nay, some of our judges speak with choked utterance and with many tears when they say to the prisoner, " You must be taken to the place from whence you came, there to be hanged by the neck till you are dead." God never puts on the black cap without his heart yearning for men. His mercy endureth for ever, and he delighteth in it.

Notice how the Lord teacheth us his care even over the most guilty by the comparisons he makes. " What man of you," says he, " having a sheep gone astray will not go after it until he find it ? What man of you having a sheep that is fallen into a ditch will not pull it out ? " Any animal which belongs to us causes us concern if we lose it, or it is in trouble. I noticed the other night how even the little kitten could not be missing without causing anxiety to the household. What calling and searching ! Rougher natures might say, " if the kitten will keep out of doors all night, let it do so." But the owner thought not so, for the night was cold and wet. I have seen great trouble when a bird has been lost through the opening of a cage door, and many a vain struggle to catch it again. What a stir there is in the house about a little short-lived animal. We do not like to lose a bird, or a kitten, and do you think the good God will willingly lose those whom he has made in his own image, and who are to exist for ever? I have used a very simple and homely illustration, but it commends itself to the heart. You know what you would do to regain a lost bird, and what will not God do to save a soul! An immortal spirit is better than ten thousand birds. Does God care for souls? Ay, that he does, and in proof thereof Jesus has come to seek and to save the lost. The Shepherd cannot rest while one : of his flock is in danger. "It is only one sheep! You have ninety-nine more, good man, why do you fret and bother yourself about one?" He cannot be pacified. He is considering where that sheep may be. He imagines all sorts of perils and distresses. Perhaps it is lying on its back, and cannot turn over, or it has fallen into a pit, or is entangled among briars, or the wolf is ready to seize it. It is not merely its intrinsic value to him, but he is concerned for it because it is *his* sheep, and the object of his care. Oh, soul, God has such a care for man. He waits to be gracious, and his Spirit goes forth towards sinners; therefore return to him.

Now dwell upon that last argument—"*He will not forget the covenant of thy fathers.*" The covenant always keeps open the path between God and man. The Lord has made a covenant concerning poor sinners with his Son Jesus Christ. He has laid help upon one that is mighty, and given him for a covenant to the people. He evermore remembers Jesus, and how he kept that covenant; he calls to mind his sighs, and tears, and groans, and death-throes, and he fulfils his promise for the great Sufferer's sake. God's grace has kept his covenant on the behalf of men: God is even eager to forgive that he may reward Christ, and give him to see of the travail of his soul. Now, hearken unto me, ye who are still unconverted. What solid ground there is here for your hope. If the Lord were to deal with you according to the covenant of works, what could he do but destroy you? But there is a covenant of grace made in Jesus Christ on the behalf of sinners, and all that believe in Jesus are interested in that covenant and are made partakers of the countless blessings which that covenant secures. Believe thou in Jesus. Cast thyself upon him, and by the covenant mercies of God thou shalt assuredly be saved.

You have heard me preach like this before, have you not, a good many times? Yes, and I am sometimes fearful lest God's people should grow tired of this kind of sermon: but then *you* need it over and over again. How many more times will some of you want to be told this? How many more times must the great mercy of God be set before you? Are we to keep on inviting you again and again and again and go back with no favourable answer from you? I have been questioning myself in the night watches about this, and I have said, "These people are unconverted, is it my fault? Do I fail in telling them my Lord's message? Do I mar the gospel?" Well, I thought, "If it be so, yet I will charge them not to be partakers of my fault." Brothers and sisters, God's mercy is so rich that, even when the story of it is badly told, it ought to influence your hearts. It is so grand a thing that God should be in Christ reconciling the world to himself by a wondrous sacrifice, that if I stuttered and stammered you ought to be glad to hear it; or even if I told you in terms that were obscure you ought to be so eager to know it that you would search out my meaning. In secret correspondence a cipher is often used, but inquisitive people soon discover it, ought there not to be yet more interest taken in the gospel? But, my friends, I do not speak obscurely. I am as plain a speaker as one might meet in a day's march, and with all my heart I set Christ before you, and bid you trust him; will you do so this morning, or will you not? See how dark it is outside, even at noon-day. God has hung the very heavens in mourning. Never fear, the sun will soon break forth and light up the day; and even so

> " Our hearts, if God we seek to know
> Shall know him, and rejoice ;
> His coming like the morn shall be,
> As morning songs his voice.
>
> So shall his presence bless our souls,
> And shed a joyful light ;
> That hallow'd morn shall chase away
> The sorrows of the night."

Our Change of Masters

"Being then made free from sin, ye became the servants of righteousness."
Romans vi. 18.

MAN was made to rule. In the divine original he was intended for a king, who should have dominion over the beasts of the field, and the fowl of the air, and the fish of the sea. He was designed to be the lord-lieutenant of this part of creation, and the form of his body and the dignity of his countenance betoken it. He walks erect among the animals, while they move upon all-fours; he subjugates and tames them to perform his will, and the fear and dread of him is upon all creatures, for they know their sovereign. Yet is it equally true that man was made to serve. At his beginning he was placed in the garden to keep it, and to dress it, and so to serve his Maker. His natural feebleness, his dependence upon rain, and sun, and dew, his instinctive awe of an unseen and omnipotent spirit, indicate that he is not the chief of the universe, but a subordinate being, whose lot it is to serve. We find within man various powers and propensities seeking to get dominion over him, so that his mind also is capable of servitude. The appetites which are essential for the sustenance of his bodily frame, even such as eating and drinking, endeavour to master him, and if they can they will do so, and reduce him below the level of the swine. Man is in part spirit, but he is also in part animal, and the animal strives to get dominion over the spiritual; and in many, many men it does so, till they are utterly degraded. Nothing can be worse than a soul enslaved by such a body as that of man. The brute nature of man is the worst sort of brute. There is no beast in wolf, or lion, or serpent that is so brutish as the beast in man. Did I not tell you last Sabbath day that whereas, according to the Levitical law, he that touched a dead animal was unclean till the evening, he who touched a dead man was unclean seven days, for man is a seven times more polluting creature than any of the beasts of the field when his animal nature rules him.

If evil aims at ruling man the good Spirit also strives with him. When God of his infinite mercy visits man by his Spirit, that Spirit does not come as a neutral power to dwell quietly within man, and to share his heart with the Prince of Darkness, but he enters with full intent to reign. Hence there is a conflict which cannot be ended by an armistice, but must be carried on to the end, and that end will be found either in the driving out of the evil or in the thrusting out of the good; for one or the other, either the Prince of Darkness or the King of Light, will have dominion over man. Man must have a master: he cannot serve two masters, but he must serve *one*. Of all sorts of men this has been true, and it has perhaps been most clearly seen in those who were evidently made to lead their fellow men: it is specially seen in such a man, for instance, as Alexander, a true king of men, so heroic and great-hearted that one does not wonder that armies were fired with enthusiasm by his presence, and drove everything before them. Alexander conquered the world, and yet on occasions he became the captive of drunkenness and the bondsman of his passionate temper. At such times the king of men, the vanquisher of armies, was little better than a raving maniac. Look for further illustration at the busts of the emperors of Rome, the masters of the world; study their faces, and mark what grovelling creatures they must have been. Rome had many slaves, but he who wore her purple was the most in bonds. No slave that ground at the mill, or died in the amphitheatre, was more in bondage than such men as Tiberius and Nero, who were the bond-slaves of their passions. High rank does not save a man from being under a mastery: neither does learning nor philosophy deliver men from this bondage, for the teachers of liberty have not themselves been free, but it has happened as the apostle saith, "While they promise them liberty they themselves are the servants of corruption." Solomon himself, with all his wisdom, played the fool exceedingly, and though he was the most sagacious ruler of his age he became for awhile completely subject to his fleshly desires.

Man is born to be a servant, and a servant he must be. *Who shall be his master?* That is the question. Our text proves the point with which I have started, for it speaks of "being made free from sin," and in the same breath it adds, "Ye became the servants of righteousness." There is no interregnum: there does not appear to be a moment left for an independent state, but out of one servitude we pass into another. Do not think I made a mistake in the use of the word servitude; I might have translated the Greek word by that of slave, and have been correct. "Being made free from sin, ye were enslaved to righteousness." The apostle makes an excuse for using the figure, and says, "I speak after the manner of men, because of the infirmity of your flesh." He did not know how else to describe it, for when we come from under the absolute power of sin we come at once into a like subjection to righteousness; as we were governed and swayed by the love of sin, so we become in a similar manner subject to the forces of grace and truth. As sin took possession of us and controlled our acts, so grace claims us as its own, takes possession of us, and rules us with an absolute sway. Man passes from one master to another, but he is always in subjection. Free will I have often heard of, but I have never seen it. I have met with will, and plenty of it, but it has either been led captive by sin or held in blessed bonds of grace. The passions drive it hither and thither like a rolling thing before a whirlwind; or the understanding sways it, and then, according as the understanding is darkened or enlightened, the will acts for good or evil. In any case the bit is in its mouth, and it is guided by a power beyond itself.

However, I leave that question, and call attention this morning first of all to *our change of masters*—" Being made free from sin, we become the servants of righteousness": secondly, to *the reasons for that change;* and thirdly, to *the consequences of that change.*

I. We begin with OUR CHANGE OF MASTERS. We must have a master, but some of us by divine grace have made a change of masters infinitely to our advantage. In describing this inward revolution we will begin with a word or two upon our old master. The apostle says in the verse preceding our text, " *Ye were the servants of sin.*" How true that is! Those of us who now believe, and are free from sin, were all without exception the servants of sin. We were not all alike enslaved, but we were all under bondage. Sin has its liveried servants. Did you ever see a man dressed in the full livery of sin? A fine suit, I warrant you! Sin clothes its slave with rags, with shame, and often with disease. When fully dressed in Satan's uniform the sinner is abominable, even to his fellow sinners. If you want to see sin's liveried servants dressed out in their best or their worst, go to the prison, and you will find them there; or go to the dens of infamy in this great city, or to the liquor-bars, or to the places of vicious amusement, and you will find them there. Many of them wear the badge of the devil's drudgery upon their backs in poverty and rags, upon their faces in the blotches born of drunkenness, and in their very bones in the consequences of their vice. Satan has regimentals for his soldiers, and they are worthy of the service.

But great folks have many servants who are out of livery, and so has sin. We were not all open transgressors before our new birth, though we were all the servants of sin. There are many slaves of evil whom you would not know to be such if you only saw the surface of their characters. They do not swear, or steal, or commit adultery, or even break the Sabbath outwardly; on the contrary, they are most moral in their conduct. They are the servants of sin, but they are secretly so, for fear of rebuke; they are non-professing sinners and yet sincerely in love with sin. They stood up and sung the hymn just now, they bowed their heads in prayer, and they are now listening to the sermon, and no one will know the difference between them and the servants of Christ by their exterior; but at heart they reject the Son of God, and refuse to believe in him, for they love the pleasures of sin and the wages of unrighteousness. A kind of selfish caution restrains them from overt acts of transgression, but their heart loves not God, and their desires are not towards his ways. O, my dear hearer, if thou art setting up thine own righteousness in thy soul as an anti-Christ against God's Christ, if thou art kicking against the sway of the Divine Spirit, if thou art secretly living in sin, if thou art following out some sweet sin in secret, even though thou darest to appear in the livery of Christ, yet still thou art the slave of sin. Hypocrites are worse slaves than any others, because they are laid under the restraints of religious men without enjoying their consolations, and they practise the sins of the ungodly without their pleasures. Every hypocrite is a fool and a coward; he has not the will to serve the Lord and yet he has not the courage to serve the devil out and out. These go-betweens are of all sorts of people the most to be pitied and the most to be blamed.

As long as we are unbelievers we are the servants of sin, but we are not all outdoor servants of sin. Sin has its domestic servants who keep quiet, as well as its soldiers who beat the drum. Many keep their sin to themselves: nobody hears of them in the street, they raise no public scandal, and yet at heart they are the faithful followers of wickedness and rebellion. Their idols are set up in secret chambers, but they are heartily loved. Their desires and aspirations are all selfish, but they try to conceal this fact even from themselves; they will not serve God, they will not bow before his Son, and yet they would shrink from avowing their rebellion. They are amiable, admirable, and excellent in their outward deportment; but they are the indoor servants of Satan for all that, and their heart is full of enmity against God. Some of us confess that it was so with us. When none found fault with us we were, nevertheless, rotten in heart. We used to pray, but it was a mockery of God; we went up to God's house, but we regarded not his word, and yet in all this we prided ourselves that we were righteous.

There are, however, many believers, who were once outdoor servants of Satan, sinning openly and in defiance of all law. I thank God that there are some here who are now the servants of Christ, upon whom I can look with great delight, although they were once the open, overt, zealous, diligent servants of the devil. Now they are washed, renewed, and sanctified. Glory be to God for it. Oh that the Lord would bring some more great sinners inside this house and turn them into great saints, for bold offenders make zealous lovers of Jesus when he puts away their sins. They love much because they have had much forgiven, and inasmuch as they desperately sinned so do they devoutly love; and their surrender to Christ is as entire and unreserved as their former surrender to the service of evil. In this let God be praised. Still, let us all humbly bow before the truth we are now speaking of, and own with great humiliation of spirit that we were the servants of sin.

In passing on we notice next the expression of the apostle, "*Being made free from sin.*" Through divine grace we have been led to trust the Lord Jesus Christ for eternal salvation, and having done so we are at this moment free from sin. Come you who trust the Saviour's name, and rejoice in the words before us, for they describe you. You *are* made free from sin—not you *shall be*, but you *are*. In what sense is this true?

First, in the sense of condemnation. The believer is no more condemned for sin. Your sin was laid on Christ of old, and he as your scapegoat took it all away. "There is therefore now no condemnation to them which are in Christ Jesus." You are acquitted and justified through the Lord your righteousness. Clap your hands for joy! It is a mercy worth ten thousand worlds. You are made free from the damning power of sin, now and for ever.

Next, you are made free from the guilt of sin. As you cannot be condemned so does the truth go further, you cannot even be accused; your transgression is forgiven you, your sin is covered. "As far as the east is from the west, so far hath he removed our transgressions from us."

"Who shall lay anything to the charge of God's elect? It is God that justifieth. Who is he that condemneth? It is Christ that died, yea rather, that is risen again, who is even at the right hand of God, who also maketh intercession for us." You are delivered from sin's guilt at this moment—"made free from sin."

You are in consequence free from the punishment of sin. You shall never be cast into hell, for Jesus has suffered in your stead, and the justice of God is satisfied. As a believer in Christ, for you there is no bottomless pit, for you no undying worm, for you no fire unquenchable; but, guilty as you are by nature, Christ hath made you so completely clean that for you is reserved the "Come, ye blessed of my Father, inherit the kingdom prepared for you before the foundation of the world."

Nor is this all. You are made free from sin as to its reigning power, and this is a point in which you greatly delight. Sin once said to you, "Go," and you went: it says "Go" now, but you do not go. Sometimes sin stands in your way when grace says "Go," and then you would gladly run but sin opposes and hinders; and yet you will not yield to its demands, for grace holds dominion. You push, you struggle, you resolve that sin shall not be lord of your life, for you are not under the law but under grace. Sin hides itself in holes and corners of your nature, skulks in the dark about the streets of Mansoul, plots and plans if it can to get the mastery over you; but it never shall: it is cast out of the throne, and the Holy Ghost sits there ruling your nature, and there he will sit until you shall be perfected in holiness, and shall be caught up to dwell with Christ for ever and ever.

"Made free from sin." I wish I could now leave off preaching, and get into a quiet pew, and sit down with you and meditate upon that thought; chewing the cud as you farmers say, and getting the juice out of this rich pasturage. "Made free from sin!" Why, as I pronounce those blessed words I feel like an escaped negro in the old slave days when he leaped upon British soil in Canada. After all his running through the woods, and crossing of hills and rivers, he was free! How he leaped for joy! How he cried with delight! Even so did we exult in our liberty when at the first our Lord Jesus set us free. You who were never slaves, and never felt the taskmaster's lash, you do not know the value of liberty; and so in spiritual things, if you have never felt the slavery of sin, and have never escaped therefrom into the good land of grace where Christ hath made you free indeed, you do not know the joy of the redeemed. I am free! I am free! I am free!—I that was once a slave to every evil desire! I am made free by omnipotent love! I have escaped from the taskmaster's fetters, and I am the Lord's free man! Let all the angels praise my redeeming Lord. Let all the spirits before the throne praise the Lord, who hath led his people out of bondage, for he is good, for his mercy endureth for ever.

Now, how came we to be free? We have become free in three ways. First, by *purchase*, for our Saviour has paid the full redemption money for us, and there is not a halfpenny due upon us. Blessed be his name, there is no mortgage on his inheritance; the price is all paid and we are Christ's unencumbered property for ever. Here we stand at this moment free, because we are ransomed, and we know that our Redeemer liveth.

Our body, soul, and spirit are all bought with a price, and in our complete manhood we are Christ's.

Next, we are free by *power* as well as by purchase. Just as the Israelites were the Lord's own people, but he had to bring them out of Egypt with a high hand and an outstretched arm, so has the Lord by power broken the neck of sin and brought us up from the dominion of the old Pharaoh of evil and set us free. The Spirit's power, the same power which raised Christ from the dead, ay, the same power which made the heavens and the earth, hath delivered us, and we are the ransomed of the Lord.

And then we are free by *privilege*. "Unto as many as believed him, to them gave he the privilege to become the sons of God." God has declared us free. His own royal, majestic, and divine decree has bidden the prisoners go forth. The Lord himself looseth the prisoners, and declares that they shall no more be held in captivity. Price and power and privilege meet together in our liberty.

How came we to be free? I will tell you another story. We are free in a strange way. According to the chapter in which we find our text we are free because *we have died*. If a slave dies his master's possession in him is ended. The tyrant can rule no longer, death has relaxed his hold. "He that is dead is free from sin." Sin comes to me and asks me why I do not obey its desires. I have a reply ready. "Ah, Master Sin, I am dead! I died some thirty years ago, and I do not belong to you any more. What have you to do with me?" Whenever the Lord brings a man to die in Christ the blessed, heavenly death unto sin, how hath sin any more dominion over him? He is clear from his old master, because he is dead. Our old master lives to us, but we do not live to him. He may make what suit he pleases, we will not acknowledge his right. Some of us have made a public claim of our freedom by death, for *we have been buried*, and the apostle saith, "Know ye not, that so many of us as were baptized into Jesus Christ were baptized into his death? Therefore we are buried with him by baptism into death: that like as Christ was raised up from the dead by the glory of the Father, even so we also should walk in newness of life." We do not trust in the burial of baptism, for we know that there would have been no truth in it if we had not been dead first; but still it is a blessed sign to us that inasmuch as we died we have also been buried. Whenever the devil comes to us we can each one say to him, "I am no servant of yours, I died and was buried, did you not see me laid in the liquid tomb?" Oh, it is a blessed thing when the Lord enables us to feel a clear assurance that our baptism was not a mere form, but the instructive token of a work within the soul wrought by the divine Spirit, which set us free from the thraldom of sin.

A third thing has happened to us: *we have risen again*. According to Paul's teaching we have risen in the resurrection of Christ: a new life has been given to us: we are new creatures in Christ Jesus. We are not the same people that we once were; old things have passed away, behold all things have become new. If some of you were to meet your old selves you would not know yourselves, would you? My old self does not know me, and cannot make me out. I am dead to him as to his reigning power, and buried too, so that I can never be his subject, nor can he ever be the king of my heart, yet he struggles to dwell within me, and seems to have as many lives as a cat. Every now and then my old self sneeringly cries to my true self, "What a fool you are." My true self answers, "No, I was a fool when you had sway, but now I have come to my right mind." Sometimes that old self whispers, "There is no reality in faith," and the new self replies, "There is no reality in the things which are seen. This world is a shadow, but heaven is eternal." "Ah," says the old self, "you are a hypocrite." "No," says the new self, "I was false when I was under your power, but now I am honest and true." Yes, brethren, we are risen with Christ: with him we died and were buried, and with him we are risen, and hence we are free. What slave would remain under the dominion of a master if he could say, "I died, sir: you cannot own me now, for your ownership only extended over one life. I was buried; did you own me when I was buried? I have risen again, and my new life is not yours; I am not the same man that I was, and you have no rights over me." We have undergone this wondrous death and resurrection, and so we can say this morning with heartfelt joy, "We are made free from sin."

We are also free from sin in our hearts: we do not love it now, but loathe the thought of it. We are free from sin as to our new nature: it cannot sin because it is born of God. We are free from sin as to God's purpose about us, for he will present us ere long blameless and faultless before his presence with exceeding great joy. We do not belong to sin; we refuse to serve sin; we are made free from it by the grace of God.

Now, the third part of this change of masters is this—"*ye became the servants of righteousness.*" So we have done, and we are now in the possession of righteousness and under its rule. A righteous God has made us die to sin: a righteous God has redeemed us: a new and and righteous life has been infused into us, and now righteousness rules and reigns in us. We do not belong to ourselves, but we yield ourselves up entirely to the Redeemer's sway through his Spirit, and the more completely he rules us the better. The text says we are enslaved to righteousness, and so we wish to be. We wish we were so enslaved that we could not even will a wrong thing nor wish an evil thing. We desire to give ourselves up wholly and absolutely to the divine sway, so that the right, and the true, and the good may hold us in perpetual bonds. We abandon ourselves to the supremacy of God, and we find our liberty in being entirely subjected to the will of the Most High. This is a change of masters with which I know that some of you are well acquainted. I am afraid, however, that others of you know nothing about it. May the Lord grant that you may be made to know it before you go to sleep to-night. May you be delivered from the black tyrant and brought into the service of the Prince of Peace, and that straightway.

II. Secondly, let us survey the REASONS FOR OUR CHANGE. How do we justify this change of masters? A man who makes frequent shifts is not good for much. But we changed our old master because he never had any right to us, and we were illegally detained by him. Why should sin have dominion over us? Sin did not make us, sin does not feed us, sin has no right to us whatever; we never owed it a moment's homage; we are not debtors to the flesh to live after the flesh. Our old master cannot summon us for desertion, for he stole our services. Besides, our old master was as bad as bad could be. You never saw his portrait; but he that would paint a picture of sin would have to put upon the canvas all the monstrosities that ever existed, and all the horrors that were ever imagined, and these would have to be exaggerated and condensed into one, before they could fairly depict the deformity of sin. Sin is worse than the devil, for sin made the devil a devil; he would have been an angel if it had not been for sin. Oh, who would serve the destroying tyrant who of old cast down even the stars of light and turned angels into fiends? We ran away from our old master because we had never any profit at his hands. The apostle says, "What fruit had he then?" Ask the drunkard, "What did you get by the drink?" Who hath woe? Who hath redness of the eyes? Ask the spendthrift what he gained by his debauchery. He would hardly like to tell you, and I certainly should not like to repeat his tale. Ask any man that lives in sin what he has gained by it, and you will find it is all loss; sin is evil and only evil, and that continually. We have found that out, and therefore we have quitted the old master, and taken up with the new. Beside that, our old master, sin, brought us shame. There was no honour in serving him. His work is called by Paul, "those things whereof ye are now ashamed." We are in the sight of God, ay, and in our own sight, ready to blush scarlet at the very thought of the evil in which we once took delight. Sin is a grovelling, mean, despicable thing, and we are ashamed of having been connected with it. Moreover, its wages are death, and this is dreadful to think upon. Sin at one time was pleasant to us, but when we found out that sin led its servants down to hell, and plunged them into fire unquenchable, we renounced its rule, and found another lord.

But why did we take up with our new Master? We could not help it, for it was he that set us free; it was he that bought us, it was he that fought for us, it was he that brought us into liberty. Ah, if you could see him you would not ask us why we became his servants. In the first place, we owe ourselves wholly to him; and in the next place, if we did not, he is so altogether lovely, so matchless, and so charming, that if we had a free choice of masters we would choose him a thousand times over, for he is the crown and glory of mankind, among the sons there is none to be compared to him.

If you want us to justify our service of him, we tell you that his service is perfect freedom and supreme delight. We have had to suffer a little sometimes when his enemy and ours has barked at us, and the ungodly have called us ill names, but we count it honour to suffer for Jesus' sake: for he is so sweet, and so good, that if we had a thousand lives, and could give each one away by a martyr's death, we count him worthy of those lives, so sweet is he to our hearts' love. Why have we taken our new Master? Why, because he gives us even now a present payment in his service. If there were no hereafter we would be satisfied with the present delight he gives us, but in addition to that he has promised us, as a future reward, life eternal at his right hand. We think, therefore, that we have more than sufficient reason for becoming the servants of Jesus Christ, who is made of God unto us righteousness. Dear hearers, how I wish that you would all enter my Lord's service by faith in his name.

III. In the third place, and very practically, I want to talk to those who are servants of God upon THE CONSEQUENCES OF THIS CHANGE. Ye have become the servants of righteousness, and the first consequence is that you belong wholly to your Lord? Have you recognized this? I know numbers of Christian people—I hope they are Christian people, for in some points they seem as if they were—but if I were asked to look at their lives, and give an opinion as to whom they belong, I should be compelled to say, "They seem mostly to belong to themselves." To whom does their property belong? "To themselves." To whom does their time belong? "To themselves." To whom does their talent belong? "To themselves." As far as I can see they lay all out upon themselves, and live for themselves. And what do they give to God? If they are rather generous they give him the candle-ends and the parings of the cheese, and little odds and ends, threepenny-bits, and things they do not want, and can give without missing them. There are hundreds of professors who never gave God anything that cost them a self-denial; no, not so much as going without a dish on the table, or a picture on the wall, or a ring on the finger. There are numbers of professing Christians who spend a deal more on the soles of their boots than on Christ, and many women who spend more on the feathers and the flowers which deck their bonnets than on their Saviour. Yes, and I have heard of men who said they were perfect, and yet they were worth half a million of money, and were hoarding up more! Sinners dying and being damned and missionaries without support, and yet these absolutely perfect men are piling up gold and letting the cause of Christ stop for means. It is not my theory of perfection, nay, it does not seem to me to come up to the idea of a common Christian who says he is not his own. If you are really saved, brethren, not a hair of your heads belongs to yourselves: Christ's blood has either bought you or it has not, and if it has, then you are altogether Christ's, every bit of you, and you are neither to eat nor drink, nor sleep, but for Christ. "Whatsoever ye do, do all to the glory of God." Have you ever got a hold of that? Just as a negro used to belong to the man that bought him, every inch of him, so you are the slave of Christ; you bear in your body the brand of the Lord Jesus, and your glory and your freedom lie therein. That is the first consequence of being set free from sin,—ye became the servants of righteousness.

What next? Why, because you are Christ's his very name is dear to you. You are not so his slave that you would escape from his service if you could; no, but you would plunge deeper and deeper into it. You want to be more and more the Lord's. His very name is sweet to you. If you meet with the poorest person who belongs to Christ you love him, and though perhaps some who are like Christ in other respects may have awkward tempers, you put up with their infirmities for his sake. Where there is anything of Christ there your love goes forth. I remember when I left the village where I first preached I felt that if I had met a dog that came from Waterbeach I should have petted him; and such is the love we have for Christ that the lowest and weakest thing that belongs to him we love for his sake: the very sound of his name is music to us, and those who do not love him we cannot endure. Haydn, the great musician, one day walked down a London street and turning into a music-seller's shop, he asked the salesman if he had any select and beautiful music?

"Well sir," said he, "I have some sublime music by Mr. Haydn." "Oh," said Haydn, "I'll have nothing to do with that." "Why, sir, you come to buy music and will have nothing to do with Mr. Haydn's composition! What fault can you find with it?" "I can find a great deal of fault with it, but I will not argue with you: I do not want any of his music." "Then," said the shopkeeper, "I have other music, but it is not for such as you," and he turned his back on him. A thorough enthusiast grows impatient of those who do not appreciate what he so much admires. If we love Jesus we shall sometimes feel an impatient desire to get away from those who know him not. You do not love Christ? What kind of man can you be to be so blind, so dead? You can be no friend of mine if you are not a friend of Christ's. I would do anything for your good, but you cannot yield me delight or be my bosom friend unless you love my Lord, for he has engrossed my heart and taken entire possession of my spirit. If you have thus become a servant of righteousness you will weary of that which does not help you in his service, but the name of your Master will be as choicest music to you.

And now, dear friends, let me mention another result. All your members are henceforth reserved for Christ. What does the apostle say? "When ye were the servants of sin ye were free from righteousness." When Satan was your master you did not care about Christ, did you? You had no respect for him, and if anybody brought the words of Jesus before you you said, "Take them away—I do not want to hear them." You went wholly in for evil. Now, just in the same way yield yourself up wholly to Christ, and say, "Now, Satan, when I was yours I did not yield obedience to Jesus, and now that I am Christ's I can yield no obedience to you." If Satan brings sin before you, say, "I cannot see it: my eyes are Christ's:" and if he would charm you with the sweet sound of temptation say, "I cannot hear it: my ears are Christ's." "Oh," saith he, "seize on this delight." You answer, "I cannot reach it; my hands are Christ's." "But taste this sweet draught," saith he. You say, "I cannot take it, my lips are Christ's, my mouth is Christ's, all my members are Christ's." "Well, but you can form a judgment, cannot you, about this error?" "No, I do not want to know anything about it; my understanding is Christ's." "Oh, but hear this new thing." "No, I do not want to hear it; I have found Christ, who is new enough for me; I do not want your novel discoveries; I am dead to them. I do not want to be worried with arguments which dishonour my Lord: take them away. When I was a servant of sin I would not meddle with the truth, and now that I am a servant of Christ I will not trifle in the opposite direction; I have done with all but Jesus."

Think, my brethren, when we were servants of sin in what way we served it; for just as we used to serve sin, so ought we to work for Jesus. I do not speak to all here present, but I speak to many who were sinners of an open kind: how did you serve sin? I will answer for them. They did not require to be egged on to it; they did not want any messenger of the devil to plead with them and urge them to unholy pleasures and unclean delights. Far from it; some even of their own companions thought them too imprudent. Now, dear friends, you ought not to want your ministers or Christian friends to stir you up to good works ; you ought to be just as eager after holiness as you were after sin. Evil was very sweet to you once. You used to watch for the day when you could indulge in a sweet sin ; did you not ? When the time was coming round when you could take a deep draught of iniquity you took the almanack and looked for it as a child for his holidays. You did not mind travelling from town to town to make a round of dissipation. Brother, serve Christ in the same way. May his Holy Spirit help you to do so. Watch for opportunities of doing good ; do not need whipping to duty. Instead of requiring to be urged forward in evil we needed holding back : did we not ? Our parents had to put the rein upon us ! Sometimes mother would say, "John, do not so," and father would cry, "My boy, do not this." We wanted a deal of restraint. I wish I had a band of Christians round me who needed holding back in the service of Christ : I have not met with that sort yet. I am prepared with any kind of curb when I meet with a high-mettled Christian, who goes at too great a rate in his Lord's service. For the most part my Master's horses are fonder of getting into the stables than out into the hunting field. I have not met with one who has done too much for the Lord. I shall never be guilty of too much work myself ; I wish I could go like the wind in serving Jesus.

Brethren, be just as hot to honour Christ as you once were to dishonour him. As you have given the devil first-rate service, let Christ have the same. You recollect in the days of your sin, some of you who went in for it thoroughly, that you never stood at any expense— did you ? Oh no, if you wanted pleasure in sin, away went the five pounds, and the hundreds. How often do I meet with men, particularly those given to drink, who get pounds in their pockets and never know how they go ; but they will never leave off till all is spent, be it little or much. Poor fools, poor fools. Yet I wish we could serve Jesus Christ thus unstintedly. No expense should be reckoned so long as we can honour him and bless his name. Bring forth the alabaster box ; break it, never mind the chips and pieces ; pour out the oil, and let Jesus have it all. It was thus I served Satan and thus would I serve Christ.

Ay, and the poor slaves of sin not only do not stop at expense, but they are not frightened by any kind of loss. See how many lose their characters for the sake of one short hour of sin. How many are wringing their hands now because none will trust them, and they are cut off from decent society because of one short-lived sin. They ruin their peace and think nothing of it. A quiet conscience is the brightest of jewels, but they fling it away to enjoy their sin. They will lose their health, too, for the sake of indulging their passions. The devil says, "Drink, drink ; drink yourselves blind ;" and they do it as eagerly as if it were for their good. They are martyrs for Satan. Never did a Zulu fling himself upon death for his king so recklessly as these servants of Satan yield themselves for his service. They will do anything ; they will destroy their health, and, what is worst of all, destroy their souls for ever for the sake of sin's brief delights. They know that there is a hell, they know that the wrath of God abideth for ever on guilty men, but they risk all and lose all for sin. In that same way should we serve our Lord. Be willing to lose character for him ; be willing to lose health for him ;

be willing to lose life for him; be willing to lose all, if by any means you may glorify him whose servant you have become.

Oh, who will be my Master's servant? Here he comes! Do you not see him? He wears upon his head no diadem but the crown of thorns; adown his cheeks you see the spittle flowing, his feet are still rubied with their wounds, and his hands are still bejewelled with the marks of the nails. This is your Master, and these are the insignia of his love for you. What service will you render him? That of a mere professor, who names his name but loves him not? That of a cold religionist, who renders unwilling service out of fear? I pray you, brethren, do not so dishonour him. I lift the standard this morning to enlist beneath the banner of Christ those who will henceforth be Christ's men from head to foot; and happy shall the church be, and happy the entire Israel of God if a chosen number shall enlist and remain true to their colours. We need no more of your nominal Christians, your lukewarm Christians, whom my Master spues out of his mouth: we need men on fire with love, all over consecrated, intensely devoted, who, by the slavery from which they have escaped, and by the liberty into which they have entered, are under bond to spend and be spent for the name of Jesus, till they have filled the earth with his glory, and made all heaven ring with his praise. The Lord bless you, beloved, for Jesus' sake. Amen.

A Summary of Experience
and a Body of Divinity

"For they themselves show of us what manner of entering in we had unto you, and how ye turned to God from idols to serve the living and true God; and to wait for his Son from heaven, whom he raised from the dead, even Jesus, which delivered us from the wrath to come."—1 Thessalonians i. 9, 10.

In Thessalonica the conversions to the faith were remarkable. Paul came there without prestige, without friends, when he was in the very lowest condition; for he had just been beaten and imprisoned at Philippi, and had fled from that city. Yet it mattered not in what condition the ambassador might be ; God, who worketh mighty things by weak instruments, blessed the word of his servant Paul. No doubt when the apostle went into the synagogue to address his own countrymen he had great hopes that, by reasoning with them out of their own Scriptures, he might convince them that Jesus was the Christ. He soon found that only a few would search the Scriptures and form a judgment on the point; but the bulk of them refused, for we read of the Jews of Berea, to whom Paul fled from Thessalonica, "These were more noble than those in Thessalonica, in that they received the word with all readiness of mind, and searched the scriptures daily, whether those things were so." Paul must have felt disappointed with his own countrymen; indeed, he had often cause to do so. His heart was affectionately warm toward them, but their hearts were very bitter towards him, reckoning him to be a pervert and an apostate. But if he seemed to fail with the Jews, it is evident that he was abundantly successful with the Gentiles. These turned from their idols to serve the living God, and their turning was so remarkable that the Jews charged Paul and Silas with turning the world upside down.

In those days there was a good deal of practical atheism abroad, and therefore the wonder was not so much that men left their idols, as that they turned unto the living God. It became a matter of talk all over the city, and the Jews in their violence helped to make the matter more notorious; for the mobs in the street and the attack upon the house

55

of Jason all stirred the thousand tongues of rumour. Everybody spoke of the sudden appearance of three poor Jews, of their remarkable teaching in the synagogue, and of the conversion of a great multitude of devout Greeks, and of the chief women not a few. It was no small thing that so many had come straight away from the worship of Jupiter and Mercury to worship the unknown God, who could not be seen, nor imaged; and to enter the kingdom of one Jesus who had been crucified. It set all Macedonia and Achaia wondering; and as with a trumpet-blast it aroused all the dwellers in those regions. Every ship that sailed from Thessalonica carried the news of the strange ferment which was moving the city; men were caring for religion, and were quitting old beliefs for a new and better faith. Thessalonica, situated on one of the great Roman roads, the centre of a large trade, thus became a centre for the gospel. Wherever there are true conversions there will be more or less of this kind of sounding forth of the gospel. It was especially so at Thessalonica; but it is truly so in every church where the Spirit of God is uplifting men from the dregs of evil, delivering them from drunkenness, and dishonesty, and uncleanness, and worldliness, and making them to become holy and earnest in the cause of the great Lord. There is sure to be a talk when grace triumphs. This talk is a great aid to the gospel: it is no small thing that men should have their attention attracted to it by its effects; for it is both natural and just that thoughtful men should judge of doctrines by their results; and if the most beneficial results follow from the preaching of the word, prejudice is disarmed, and the most violent objectors are silenced.

You will notice that in this general talk the converts and the preachers were greatly mixed up:—"For they themselves show of us what manner of entering in we had unto you." I do not know that it is possible for the preacher to keep himself distinct from those who profess to be converted by him. He is gladly one with them in love to their souls, but he would have it remembered that he cannot be responsible for all their actions. Those who profess to have been converted under any ministry have it in their power to damage that ministry far more than any adversaries can do. "There!" says the world, when it detects a false professor, "this is what comes of such preaching." They judge unfairly, I know; but most men are in a great hurry, and will not examine the logic of their opponents; while many others are so eager to judge unfavourably, that a very little truth, or only a bare report, suffices to condemn both the minister and his doctrine. Every man that lives unto God with purity of life brings honour to the gospel which converted him, to the community to which he belongs, and to the preaching by which he was brought to the knowledge of the truth; but the reverse is equally true in the case of unworthy adherents. Members of churches, will you kindly think of this? Your ministers share the blame of your ill conduct if ever you disgrace yourselves. I feel sure that none of you wish to bring shame and trouble upon your pastors, however careless you may be about your own reputations. Oh, that we could be freed from those of whom Paul says, "Many walk, of whom I have told you often, and now tell you even weeping, that they are the enemies of the cross of Christ : whose end is destruction, whose God is their belly, and whose glory is in their shame, who mind earthly things." When these are in a church they are its curse. The Thessalonians were not such : they were such a people that Paul did not blush to have himself implicated in what they did. He was glad to say that the outsiders " show of us what manner of entering in we had unto you, and how ye turned to God from idols, to serve the living and true God, and to wait for his Son from heaven."

Quitting this line of thought, I would observe that these two verses struck me as being singularly full. Oceans of teaching are to be found in them. A father of the church in the first ages was wont to cry, " I adore the infinity of Holy Scripture." That remark constantly rises from my lips when I am studying the sacred Word. This book is more than a book,—it is the mother of books, a mine of truth, a mountain of meaning. It was an ill-advised opinion which is imputed to the Mahommedans at the destruction of the Alexandrian Library, when they argued that everything that was good in it was already in the Koran, and therefore it might well be destroyed. Yet it is true with regard to the inspired Word of God, that it contains everything which appertains to eternal life. It is a revelation of which no man can take the measure, it compasses heaven and earth, time and eternity. The best evidence of its being written by an Infinite mind is its own infinity. Within a few of its words there lie hidden immeasurable meanings, even as perfume enough to sweeten leagues of space may be condensed into a few drops of otto of roses.

The first part of my text contains *a summary of Christian experience ;* and the second part contains *a body of divinity.* Here is ample room and verge enough. It is not possible to exhaust such a theme.

I. The first part of the text contains A SUMMARY OF EXPERIENCE : " What manner of entering in we had unto you, and how ye turned to God from idols to serve the living and true God, and to wait for his Son from heaven." Here we have in miniature the biography of a Christian man.

It begins, first, with *the entering in of the word,*—" What manner of entering in we had unto you." When we preach the word you listen, and, so far, the word is received. This is a very hopeful circumstance. Still, the hearing with the outward ear is comparatively a small matter ; or, at least, only great because of what may follow from it. The preacher feels even with some who listen with attention that he is outside the door ; he is knocking, and he hopes that he is heard within ; but the truth is not yet received, the door remains shut, an entrance is not granted, and in no case can he be content to speak with the person outside the door ; he desires an entrance for the Word. All is fruitless until Christ entereth into the heart. I have seen the following : the door has been a little opened, and the man inside has come to look at the messenger, and more distinctly to hear what he may have to say ; but he has taken care to put the door on the chain, or hold it with his hand, for he is not yet ready to admit the guest who is so desirous of entertainment. The King's messenger has sometimes tried to put his foot within when the door has stood a little open, but he has not always been successful, and has not even escaped from a painful hurt when the door has been forced back with angry violence. We have called again and again with our message, but we have been as men who besieged a walled city, and were driven from the gates; yet we had our reward, for when the Holy Spirit sweetly moved the hard heart the city gates have opened of their own accord, and we have been received joyfully. We have heard the hearty cry, "Let the truth come in! Let the gospel come in! Let Christ come in! Whatever there is in him we are willing to receive; whatever he demands we are willing to give; whatever he offers us we are glad to accept. Come and welcome! The guest-chamber is prepared. Come and abide in our house for ever!"

The truth has its own ways of entrance; but in general it first affects the understanding. The man says, "I see it: I see how God is just, and yet the Justifier of him that believeth in Jesus. I see sin laid on Christ that it may not be laid on me, and I perceive that if I believe in Jesus Christ my sins are put away by his atonement." To many all that is wanted is that they should understand this fundamental truth; for their minds are prepared of God to receive it. Only make it plain and they catch at it as a hungry man at a piece of bread. They discover in the gospel of our Lord Jesus the very thing for which they have been looking for years, and so the truth enters by the door of the understanding.

Then it usually commences to work upon the conscience, conscience being the understanding exercised upon moral truth. The man sees himself a sinner, discovering guilt that he was not aware of; and he is thus made ready to receive Christ's pardoning grace. He sees that to have lived without thinking of God, without loving God, without serving God was a great and grievous crime: he feels the offensiveness of this neglect. He trembles; he consents unto the law that it is good, and he allows that, if the law condemns him, he is worthy to be condemned.

When it has thus entered into the understanding and affected the conscience, the word of God usually arouses the emotions. Fear is awakened, and hope is excited. The man begins to feel as he never felt before. His whole manhood is brought under the heavenly spell; his very flesh doth creep in harmony with the amazement of his soul. He wonders and dreads, weeps and quivers, hopes and doubts; but no emotion is asleep; life is in all. When a tear rises to his eye he brushes it away, but it is soon succeeded by another. Repentance calls forth one after another of these her sentinels. The proud man is broken down; the hard man is softened. The love of God in providing a Saviour, the unsearchable riches of divine grace in passing by transgression, iniquity, and sin,—these things amaze and overwhelm the penitent. He finds himself suddenly dissolved, where aforetime he was hard as adamant; for the word is entering into him, and exercising its softening power.

By-and-by the entrance is complete; for the truth carries the central castle of Mansoul, and captures his heart. He who once hated the gospel now loves it. At first he loves it, hoping that it may be his, though fearing the reverse; yet owning that if it brought no blessing to himself, yet it was a lovable and desirable thing. By-and-by the man ventures to grasp it, encouraged by the word that bids him lay hold on eternal life. One who in digging his land finds a treasure, first looks about for fear lest some one else should claim it; anon he dares to examine his prize more carefully, and at length he bears it in his bosom to his own home. So is it with the gospel; when a man finds it by the understanding, he soon embraces it with his heart; and, believe me, if it once gets into the heart, the arch-enemy himself will never get it out again. Oh, that such an entrance with the gospel might commence the spiritual life of all here present who are as yet unsaved.

What comes next? Well, the second stage is *conversion.* "They themselves show of us what manner of entering in we had unto you, and how *ye turned* from idols to serve the living and true God." There came a turning, a decided turning. The man has come so far in carelessness, so far in sin and unbelief; but now he pauses, and he deliberately turns round, and faces in that direction to which hitherto he had turned his back. Conversion is the turning of a man completely round, to hate what he loved and to love what he hated. Conversion is to turn to God decidedly and distinctly by an act and deed of the mind and will. In some senses we are *turned;* but in others, like these Thessalonians, we *turn.* It is not conversion to think that you will turn, or to promise that you will turn, or resolve that you will turn, but actually and in very deed to turn, because the word has had a true entrance into your heart. You must not be content with a reformation; there must be a revolution: old thrones must fall, and a new king must reign. Is it so with you?

These Thessalonians turned from their idols. Do you tell me that you have no idols? Think again, and you will not be quite so sure. The streets of London are full of fetich worship, and almost every dwelling is a joss-house crammed with idols. Why, multitudes of men are worshipping not calves of gold, but gold in a more portable shape. Small circular idols of gold and silver are much sought after. They are very devoutly worshipped by some, and great things are said concerning their power. I have heard the epithet of "almighty" ascribed to an American form of these idols. Those who do not worship gold may yet worship rank, name, pleasure, or honour. Most worship self, and I do not know that there is a more degrading form of worship than for a man to put himself upon a pedestal and bow down thereto and worship it. You might just as well adore cats and crocodiles with the ancient Egyptians as pay your life's homage to yourselves. No wooden image set up by the most savage tribe can be more ugly or degrading than our idol when we adore ourselves. Men worship Bacchus still. Do not tell me they do not: why, there is a temple to him at every street corner. While every other trade is content with a shop or a warehouse, this fiend has his palaces, in which plentiful libations are poured forth in his honour. The gods of unchastity and vice are yet among us. It would be a shame even to speak of the things which are done of them in secret. The lusts of the flesh are served even by many who would not like to have it known. We have gods many and lords many in this land. God grant that we may see, through the preaching of the gospel, many turning from such idols. If you love anything better than God you are idolaters: if there is anything you would not give up for God it is your idol: if there is anything that you seek with greater fervour than you seek the glory of God, that is your idol, and conversion means a turning from every idol.

But then that is not enough, for some men turn from one idol to another. If they do not worship Bacchus they become teetotalers, and possibly they worship the golden calf, and become covetous. When men quit covetousness they sometimes turn to profligacy. A change of false gods is not the change that will save : we must turn unto God, to trust, love, and honour him, and him alone.

After conversion comes *service*. True conversion causes us " to serve the living and true God." To serve him means to worship him, to obey him, to consecrate one's entire being to his honour and glory, and to be his devoted servant.

We are, dear friends, to serve the " living " God. Many men have a dead God still. They do not feel that he hears their prayers, they do not feel the power of his Spirit moving upon their hearts and lives. They never take the Lord into their calculations ; he never fills them with joy, nor even depresses them with fear ; God is unreal and inactive to them. But the true convert turns to the living God, who is everywhere, and whose presence affects him at every point of his being. This God he is to worship, obey, and serve.

Then it is added, to serve the *true* God ; and there is no serving a true God with falsehood. Many evidently serve a false god, for they utter words of prayer without their hearts, and that is false prayer, unfit for the true God, who must be worshipped in spirit and in truth. When men's lives are false and artificial they are not a fit service for the God of truth. A life is false when it is not the true outcome of the soul, when it is fashioned by custom, ruled by observation, restrained by selfish motives, and governed by the love of human approbation. What a man does against his will is not in truth done by himself at all. If the will is not changed the man is not converted, and his religious life is not true. He that serves the true God acceptably does it with delight ; to him sin is misery, and holiness is happiness. This is the sort of service which we desire our converts to render : we long to see rebels become sons. Oh the sacred alchemy of the Holy Spirit, who can turn men from being the slaves of sin to become servants of righteousness !

Carefully notice the order of life's progress : the entering in of the word produces conversion, and this produces service. Do not put those things out of their places. If you are converts without the word entering into you, you are unconverted ; and if professing to receive the word you are not turned by it, you have not received it. If you claim to be converted, and yet do not serve God, you are not converted ; and if you boast of serving God without being converted, you are not serving God. The three things are links which draw on each other.

A fourth matter follows to complete this Christian biography, namely, *waiting*—"To wait for his Son from heaven." That conversion which is not followed up by waiting is a false conversion, and will come to nothing. We wait, dear brethren, in the holy perseverance of faith ; having begun with Christ Jesus our Lord we abide in him ; we trust, and then we wait. We do not look upon salvation as a thing which requires a few minutes of faith, and then all is over ; salvation is the business of our lives. We receive salvation in an instant, but we work it out with fear and trembling all our days. He that is saved continues to be saved, and goes on to be saved from day to day, from every sin and from every form of evil. We must wait upon the Lord, and renew the strength of the life which he has imparted. As a servant waiteth on her mistress, or a courtier upon his king, so must we wait upon the Lord.

This waiting also takes the shape of living in the future. A man who waits is not living on the wages of to-day, but on the recompenses of a time which is yet to come; and this is the mark of the Christian, that his life is spent in eternity rather than in time, and his citizenship is not of earth but of heaven. He has received a believing expectancy which makes him both watch and wait. He expects that the Lord Jesus will come a second time, and that speedily. He has read of his going up into heaven, and he believes it; and he knows that he will so come in like manner as he went up into heaven. For the second advent he looks with calm hope: he does not know when it may be, but he keeps himself on the watch as a servant who waits his lord's return. He hopes it may be to-day, he would not wonder if it were to-morrow, for he is always looking for and hasting unto the coming of the Son of God. The coming of the Lord is his expected reward. He does not expect to be rewarded by men, or even to be rewarded of God with temporal things in this life, for he has set his affection upon things yet to be revealed, things eternal and infinite. In the day when the Christ shall come, and the heavens which have received him shall restore him to our earth, he shall judge the world in righteousness, and his people with his truth, and then shall our day break and our shadows flee away. The true believer lives in this near future; his hopes are with Jesus on his throne, with Jesus crowned before an assembled universe.

The convert has come to this condition, he is assured of his salvation. See how he has been rising from the time when he first held the door ajar! He is assured of his salvation; for Paul describes him as one who is delivered from the wrath to come; and therefore he looks with holy delight to the coming of the Lord Jesus Christ. Once he was afraid of this, for he feared that he would come to condemn him; but now he knows that when the Lord appears his justification will be made plain to the eyes of all men. "Then shall the righteous shine forth as the sun, in the kingdom of their Father." And so he cries, "Even so, come Lord Jesus!" He would hasten rather than delay the appearing of the Lord. He groans in sympathy with travailing creation for the manifestation of the sons of God. He cries with all the redeemed host for the day of the Saviour's glory. He could not do this were he not abundantly assured that the day would not seal his destruction, but reveal his full salvation.

Here, then, you have the story of the Christian man briefly summed up, and I think you will not find a passage of merely human writing which contains so much in so small a compass. It has unspeakable wealth packed away into a narrow casket. Do you understand it? Is this the outline of your life? If it is not, the Lord grant that his word may have an entrance into you this morning, that you may now believe in Jesus Christ and then wait for his glorious appearing.

II. I shall want you to be patient with me while I very briefly unfold the second half of this great roll. Here even to a greater degree we have *multum in parvo*, much in little; A BODY OF DIVINITY packed away in a nutshell. "To wait for his Son from heaven, whom he raised from the dead, even Jesus, which delivered us from the wrath to come."

To begin my body of divinity, I see here, first, *the Deity of Christ.* "To wait for his Son." "His Son." God has but one Son in the highest sense. The Lord Jesus Christ has given to all believers power to become the sons of God, but not in the sense in which he, and he alone, is the Son of God. "Unto which of the angels said he at any time, Thou art my Son, this day have I begotten thee?" "When he bringeth in the First-begotten into the world he saith, Let all the angels of God worship him." The Eternal Filiation is a mystery into which it is better for us never to pry. Believe it; but how it is, or how it could be, certainly it is not for you or for me to attempt to explain. There is one "Son of the Highest," who is "God, of the substance of the Father, begotten before all worlds," whom we with all our souls adore, and own to be most truly God; doing so especially every time in the benediction we associate him with the Father and with the Holy Spirit as the one God of blessing.

Side by side with this in this text of mine is *his humanity.* "His Son, whom he raised from the dead." It is for man to die. God absolutely considered dieth not; he therefore took upon himself our mortal frame, and was made in fashion as a man; then willingly for our sakes he underwent the pangs of death, and being crucified, was dead, and so was buried, even as the rest of the dead. He was truly man, "of a reasonable soul, and human flesh subsisting": of that we are confident. There has been no discussion upon that point in these modern times, but there was much questioning thereon in years long gone; for what is there so clear that men will not doubt it or mystify it? With us there is no question either as to his Deity, which fills us with reverence; or his manhood, which inspires us with joy. He is the Son of God and the Son of Mary. He, as God, is "immortal, invisible"; and yet for our sakes he was seen of men and angels, and in mortal agony yielded up the ghost. He suffered for our salvation, died upon the cross, and was buried in the tomb of Joseph of Arimathæa, being verily and truly man.

Notice a third doctrine which is here, and that is *the unity of the Divine Person of our Lord;* for while the apostle speaks of Christ as God's Son from heaven, and as one who had died, he adds, "even Jesus": that is to say, one known, undivided Person. Although he be God and man, yet he is not two, but one Christ. There is but one Person of our blessed and adorable Lord: "one altogether; not by confusion of substance, but by unity of Person." He is God, he is man; perfect God and perfect man; and, as such, Jesus Christ, the one Mediator between God and man. There have been mistakes about this also made in the church, though I trust not by any one of us here present. We worship the Lord Jesus Christ in the unity of his divine Person as the one Saviour of men.

Furthermore, in our text we perceive a doctrine about ourselves very plainly implied, namely, that *men by nature are guilty,* for otherwise they would not have needed Jesus, a Saviour. They were lost, and so he who came from heaven to earth bore the name of Jesus, "for he shall save his people from their sins." It is clear, my brethren, that we were under the divine wrath, otherwise it could not be said, " He hath delivered us from the wrath to come." We who are now delivered were once "children of wrath, even as others." And when we are delivered it is a meet song to sing, "O Lord, I will praise thee: though thou wast angry with me, thine anger is turned away, and thou comfortedst me." We were guilty, else we had not needed a propitiation by the Saviour's death : we were lost, else we had not needed one who should seek and save that which is lost; and we were hopelessly lost, otherwise God himself would not have shared our nature to work the mighty work of our redemption. That truth is in the text, and a great deal more than I can mention just now.

But the next doctrine, which is one of the fundamentals of the gospel, is that *the Lord Jesus Christ died for these fallen men.* He could not have been raised from the dead if he had not died. That death was painful, and ignominious; and it was also substitutionary : "for the transgression of my people was he stricken." In the death of Christ lay the essence of our redemption. I would not have you dissociate his life from his death, it comes into his death as an integral part of it; for as the moment we begin to live we, in a sense, begin to die, so the Man of Sorrows lived a dying life, which was all preparatory to his passion. He lived to die, panting for the baptism wherewith he was to be baptized, and reaching forward to it. But it was especially, though not only, by his death upon the cross that Jesus put away our sin. Without shedding of blood there is no remission of sin. Not even the tears of Christ, nor the labours of Christ could have redeemed us if he had not given himself for us an offering and a sacrifice. " Die he, or justice must," or man must die. It was his bowing the head and giving up of the ghost which finished the whole work. " It is finished " could not have been uttered except by a bleeding, dying Christ. His death is our life. Let us always dwell upon that central truth, and when we are preaching Christ risen, Christ reigning, or Christ coming, let us never so preach any of them as to overshadow Christ crucified. "We preach Christ crucified." Some have put up as their ensign, "We preach Christ glorified"; and we also preach the same ; but yet to us it seems that the first and foremost view of Jesus by the sinner is as the Lamb of God which taketh away the sin of the world. Therefore do we preach first Christ crucified, while at the same time we do not forget that blessed hope of the child of God,—namely, Christ in glory soon to descend from heaven.

The next doctrine I see in my text is *the acceptance of the death of Christ by the Father.* "Where is that ?" say you. Look ! "Whom he raised from the dead." Not only did Jesus rise from the dead, but the Father had a distinct hand therein. God as God gave the token of his acceptance of Christ's sacrifice by raising him from the dead. It is true, as we sometimes sing,

> "If Jesus had not paid the debt,
> He ne'er had been at freedom set."

The Surety would have been held in prison to this day if he had not discharged his suretyship engagements, and wiped out all the liabilities of his people. Therefore it is written, "He was delivered for our offences, and was raised again for our justification." In his glorious uprising from the dead lies the assurance that we are accepted, accepted in the Beloved : the Beloved being himself certainly accepted because God brought him again from the dead.

Further on, we have another doctrine, among many more. We have here the doctrine of *our Lord's resurrection,* of which we spake when we mentioned the acceptance of his offering. Christ is risen from the dead. I pray you, do not think of the Lord Jesus Christ as though he were now dead. It is well to dwell upon Gethsemane, Golgotha, and Gabbatha ; but pray remember the empty tomb, Emmaus, Galilee, and Olivet. It is not well to think of Jesus as for ever on the cross or in the tomb. "He is not here, but he is risen." Ye may "come and see the place where the Lord lay," but he lies there no longer ; he hath burst the bands of death by which he could not be holden ; for it was not possible that God's holy One could see corruption. The rising of Jesus from the dead is that fact of facts which establishes Christianity upon an historical basis, and at the same time guarantees to all believers their own resurrection from the dead. He is the firstfruits and we are the harvest.

Further, there is here the doctrine of *his ascension* : "to wait for his Son from heaven." It is clear that Jesus is in heaven, or he could not come from it. He has gone before us as our Forerunner. He has gone to his rest and reward; a cloud received him out of sight; he has entered into his glory.

I doubt not our poet is right when he says of the angels—

> "They brought his chariot from on high,
>   To bear him to his throne ;
> Clapped their triumphant wings and cried,
>   'The glorious work is done!'"

That ascension of his brought us the Holy Spirit. He "led captivity captive, and received gifts for men," and he gave the Holy Ghost as the largess of his joyous entry to his Father's courts, that man on earth might share in the joy of the Conqueror returning from the battle. "Lift up your heads, O ye gates; and be ye lift up, ye everlasting doors; and the King of glory shall come in," was the song of that bright day.

But the text tells us more : not only that he has gone into heaven, but that *he remains there ;* for these Thessalonians were expecting him to come "from heaven," and therefore he was there. What is he doing? "I go to prepare a place for you." What is he doing? He is interceding with authority before the throne. What is he doing? He is from yonder hill-top looking upon his church, which is as a ship upon the sea buffeted by many a storm. In the middle watch ye shall see him walking on the waters ; for he perceives the straining of the oars, the leakage of the timbers, the rending of the sails, the dismay of the pilot, the trembling of the crew; and he will come unto us, and save us. He is sending heavenly succours to his weary ones ; he is ruling all things for the salvation of his elect, and the accomplishment of his purposes. Glory be to his blessed name!

Jesus is in heaven with saving power, too, and that also is in the text : " His Son from heaven, even Jesus, which delivereth us from the wrath to come." I alter the translation, for it is a present participle in the case of each verb, and should run, " Even Jesus, delivering us from the wrath coming." He is at this moment delivering. " Wherefore also he is able to save them to the uttermost that come unto God by him, seeing he ever liveth to make intercession for them." He is away in heaven, but he is not divided from us ; he is working here the better because he is there. He has not separated himself from the service and the conflict here below ; but he has taken the post from which he can best observe and aid. Like some great commander who in the day of battle commands a view of the field, and continues watching, directing, and so winning the fight, so is Jesus in the best place for helping us. Jesus is the master of legions, bidding his angels fly hither and thither, where their spiritual help is needed. My faith sees him securing victory in the midst of the earth. My God, my King, thou art working all things gloriously from thy vantage ground, and ere long the groans and strifes of battle shall end in Hallelujahs unto the Lord God Omnipotent ! Christ's residence in the heavens is clearly in the text.

Here is conspicuously set forth *the second coming,* a subject which might well have occupied all our time,—" To wait for his Son from heaven." Every chapter of this epistle closes with the Second Advent. Do not deceive yourselves, oh ye ungodly men who think little of Jesus of Nazareth ! The day will come when you will change your minds about him. As surely as he died, he lives, and as surely as he lives he will come to this earth again ! With an innumerable company of angels, with blast of trumpet that shall strike dismay into the heart of all his enemies, Jesus comes ! And when he cometh there shall be a time of judgment, and the rising again of the dead, and " Every eye shall see him, and they also which pierced him : and all the kindreds of the earth shall wail because of him." He may come to-morrow ! We know not the times and the seasons ; these things are in the Father's keeping ; but that he comes is certain, and that he will come as a thief in the night to the ungodly is certain too. Lay no flattering unction to your souls as though when he was crucified there was an end of him ; it is but the beginning of his dealings with you, though you reject him. " Kiss the Son, lest he be angry, and ye perish from the way, when his wrath is kindled but a little. Blessed are all they that put their trust in him."

A further doctrine in the text is that *Christ is a deliverer*—" Jesus delivering us from the wrath coming." What a blessed name is this ! Deliverer ! Press the cheering title to your breast. He delivereth by himself bearing the punishment of sin. He has delivered, he is delivering, he always will deliver them that put their trust in him.

But there was something to be delivered from, and that is, *the coming wrath,* which is mentioned here. " Oh," saith one, " that is a long way off, that wrath to come !" If it were a long way off it were wise for you to prepare for it. He is unsafe who will be destroyed most certainly, however distant that destruction may be. A wise man should not be content with looking as an ox doth, as far as his eye can carry him, for there is so much beyond, as sure as that which is seen. But it is not far-off wrath which is here mentioned ; the text saith, " who delivereth us from the wrath coming"; that is, the wrath which is now coming; for wrath is even now upon the unbelieving. As for those Jews who had rejected Christ, the apostle says of them in the sixteenth verse of the next chapter, "Forbidding us to speak to the Gentiles that they might be saved, to fill up their sins alway: for the wrath is come upon them to the uttermost." The siege of Jerusalem, and the blindness of Israel, are a terrible comment upon these words. "Indignation and wrath, tribulation and anguish, upon every soul of man that doeth evil, of the Jew first, and also of the Gentile." It is said of every one that believeth not in Christ Jesus, that "the wrath of God abideth on him." "God is angry with the wicked every day." This wrath abideth upon some of you. It is the joy of believers that they are delivered from this wrath which is daily coming upon unbelievers, and would come upon themselves if they had not been delivered from it by the atoning sacrifice.

There is evidently in the text the doctrine of *a great division* between men and men. "He hath delivered *us*." All men have not faith, and therefore all men are not delivered from wrath. To-day there is such a division; the "condemned-already" and the "justified" are living side by side; but ere long the separation shall be more apparent. While some will go away into everlasting punishment, the people of God will be found pardoned and absolved, and so will be glorified for ever.

Lastly, there is here the doctrine of *assurance*. Some say, "How are you to know that you are saved?" It can be known; it ought to be known. "Surely," cries one, "it is presumption to say that you are sure." It is presumption to live without knowing that you are delivered from wrath. Here the apostle speaks of it as a thing well known, that "Jesus delivers us from the wrath coming." He does not say "if," or "perhaps," but he writes that it is so, and therefore he knew it, and we may know it. My brother, you may know that you are saved. "That would make me inexpressibly happy," cries one. Just so, and that is one of the reasons why we would have you know it this day. God saith, "He that believeth in him hath everlasting life," and therefore the believer may be sure that he has it. Our message is, "He that believeth and is baptized shall be saved; but he that believeth not shall be damned." God make you to escape that dreadful doom! May you be delivered from the wrath which is coming for Jesus' sake. Amen.

Song for the Free, and Hope for the Bound

"He brought them out of darkness and the shadow of death, and brake their bands in sunder. Oh that men would praise the Lord for his goodness, and for his wonderful works to the children of men! For he hath broken the gates of brass, and cut the bars of iron in sunder."—Psalm cvii. 14—16.

MY anxious, prayerful desire this morning is, that some who have been in the condition described in the text may come out of it into full redemption. They have been too long in prison; and now the silver trumpet sounds—liberty to the captives. Jesus has come into the world to break the gate of brass, and to cut the bars of iron in sunder. Oh, that my prayer might be heard for those who are in bondage! I trust that some of those who are now immured in the dungeon of despondency will say "Amen" to my prayer; and if they are praying inside, and we are praying outside, and the Lord Jesus Christ himself comes to open the prison doors, then there will be a Jubilee before long.

This passage, of course, literally alludes to prisoners held in durance by their fellow-men. What a sad world man has made this earth! With superfluity of naughtiness man has multiplied his Bastilles! As if there were not misery enough to the free, he invents cells and chains! One's blood boils when standing in those living graves in which tyrants have buried their victims out of sight and hearing! Could the most fierce of wild beasts display such cruelty to their kind as men have shown to men? By the horrors of such imprisonments one must estimate the joy of being set free. To God it is a glory that, in the order of his providence, he often provides a way of escape for the oppressed. Cruel dynasties have been overthrown, tyrants have been hurled from their thrones, and then enlargement has come to those who were straitly shut up. Liberated ones should indeed "praise the Lord for his goodness, and for his wonderful works to the children of men."

But the various scenes in this Psalm were intended to describe spiritual conditions. The second verse is a key to the whole song: "Let the redeemed of the Lord say so." The deliverance here intended is one which is brought to us by redemption, and comes by the way of the great sacrifice upon Calvary. We are redeemed with the precious blood of him who surrendered his own liberty for our sakes, and consented to be bound and crucified that he might set us free. My grateful heart seems to hear him saying again, as he did in the garden of Gethsemane, "If ye seek me, let these go their way." His consenting to be bound brought freedom to all those who put their trust in him.

I shall endeavour, as God shall help me, to speak of the text spiritually, and we will consider it under the heading of three questions : first, *Who are the favoured men of whom the text speaks?* Secondly, *How has this remarkable deliverance been wrought?* Thirdly, *What shall be done about it?* The text tells us how to act. "Oh that men would praise the Lord for his goodness!"

I. First, let us ask: WHO ARE THESE FAVOURED MEN ?

These favoured persons were guilty men, as you will see by the context—" Because they rebelled against the words of God, and contemned the counsel of the Most High." Hear this, ye sinful ones, and take heart ! God has wrought great wonders for a people whom it seemed impossible for him to notice. If they came into prison through rebellion, you would expect him to leave them there. Yet rebels are set free by an act of immeasurable grace. The Redeemer has received gifts for men, "yea, for the rebellious also." These men were despisers of God's word ; was there a gospel of freedom for them ? Yes. It is for them that Jehovah, in abounding grace, has wrought miracles of mercy.

The persons described by the Psalmist were guilty of overt acts : they were in actual rebellion against the commands of the Most High. Their rebellion was not a single hasty act ; their entire lives were a continuance of their wicked revolt. From their childhood they went astray ; in their youth they provoked the Lord ; and in their manhood they disobeyed him more and more. They were in open opposition to their Creator, Benefactor, and Lord. I have no doubt that I am speaking to many who must own that they have been actual and wilful transgressors against the Lord of love. They have turned unto him the back, and not the face : they have not been servants, but rebels.

The persons here spoken of were as evil in their hearts as in their lives, for they "contemned the counsel of the Most High." Perhaps they intellectually rejected the teaching of Holy Scripture, and scorned to receive what the Lord revealed. They refused to yield their understandings to infallible teaching ; but judged their own thoughts to be better than the thoughts of God. The counsel of the Most High, though marked by the sublimity of him from whom it came, appeared to them to be less high than their own soaring theories ; and therefore they despised it. To some men any doctrine is more acceptable than that of Scripture. They gladly hear what doubters say, but they will not hear what God the Lord shall speak. His counsel of instruction, his counsel of command, his counsel of promise—his whole counsel they cast away from them, and they take counsel of their own conceit.

Now this actual and mental sin, when it is brought home to a man's awakened conscience, fills him with dismay. Because he has transgressed with hand and heart, the convinced sinner is in sore dismay. O my hearer, are you in distress this day through your own fault ? Do you wonder that you are in trouble? Did you expect to go in the way of evil, and yet to be happy? Did you never hear those words, "There is no peace, saith my God, unto the wicked"? Know you not that they are "like the troubled sea when it cannot rest, whose waters cast up mire and dirt"? Now that you find yourself taken in the thorns of your own folly, are you at all surprised? The Scripture saith, "Hast thou not procured this unto thyself?" Are not these the wages of sin? Thank God you have not yet received more than the earnest-money of that terrible wage: but, depend upon it, sin is a hard pay-master. Sin and sorrow are wedded in the very nature of things, and there is no dividing them. They that sow iniquity shall reap the same. Turn as it may, the river of wickedness at last falls into the sea of wrath. He that sins must smart unless a Saviour can be found to be his Surety, and to smart for him.

So, then, these people who were set free were by nature guilty men, who could not have deserved the divine interposition. Hear this, ye consciously guilty, you that are condemning yourselves, and confessing your faults! This is good news for you, even for you. The Lord sets free the men whose own hands have forged their manacles. This is free grace indeed! These marvels of delivering love were performed, not for the innocent in their misfortune, but for the guilty in their rebellion. "Jesus Christ came into the world to save sinners."

Go a little further, and you will notice that *these persons were doomed men,* for they "sat in darkness, and in the shadow of death." It means that they were in the condemned cell, waiting for execution. No light could come to them, for their condemnation was clear; no escape could be hoped for, not a ray of hope came from any direction. In a short time they must be taken out to execution, so that the shadow of their death fell with its damp, dread, deadening influence upon their spirits. Do I address any such this morning? Ah, my friend, I can sympathize with you as you sit here, and feel that you are doomed! I, too, have felt that sentence of death within me. I knew myself to be "condemned already," because I had not believed on the Son of God. I recollect how those words "condemned already" rang in my ears, as I should think the bell of St. Sepulchre's used to sound in the ears of the condemned in Newgate, warning them that the time was come to go out upon the scaffold. When the shadow of eternal wrath falls upon the heart, nothing worse can be imagined; for the conscience bears sure witness that God is just when he judges, condemns, and punishes. When a man feels the shadow of death upon him, infidel arguments are silenced, self-conceited defences are banished, and the heart consents to the justice of the law which declares, "The soul that sinneth, it shall die." My brethren, who remember being in this state of conscious condemnation, will join me in praying for those who are now in that condition, for they need our pity and love. O my hearers, condemned in your own consciences, take heart, and hope; for you are the sort of people whom Jehovah in his grace delights to set free! Those doomed ones were the men of whom our text sings, "He brought them out of darkness and the shadow of death." It is your condemned condition which needs free mercy; and, behold, the Lord meets your need in his boundless grace! To the doomed the Lord God in Christ Jesus will give free pardon this morning. I speak with great confidence, for my trust is in the God of love. The Lord is going to hear prayer for you, sinners. You shall be brought from under the black cloud which now threatens you with overwhelming tempest; you shall come forth from the condemned cell, not to execution, but to absolution. Blessed be the name of the Lord, he passeth by transgression, and doth it justly through the atonement of his Son!

But next, *these persons were bound men;* for they "sat in darkness and in the shadow of death, being bound in affliction and iron." Their afflictions were like iron, hard and cold, and such they could not break from. The iron entered into their souls; the rust fretted the flesh, and poisoned the blood. They were bound in a double sense : affliction within, and iron without. It is a terrible thing when a man feels that he is lost, and that he cannot get away from destruction. An evil habit has got him within its iron grasp, and will not relax its hold. Even though he would, he cannot loose himself from the thraldom of his sin. He has become a slave, and there is no escape for him. "O my God!" he cries, "what can I do?" The more he strains, the faster the iron seems to hold him. His attempts to be free from evil only prove to him how much enslaved he is. What an awful compound is described in the text—"affliction and iron"! The bondage is mental and physical too. The enslaved spirit and the depraved flesh act and react upon each other, and hold the poor struggling creature as in an iron net. He cannot break off his sins, he cannot rise to a better life. I know that some of you who are here at this time are in this case. You long to be delivered, but you are unable to cut the cords which hold you. You are greatly troubled day after day, and cannot rest; and yet you get no further. You are striving to find peace, but peace does not come; you are labouring after emancipation from evil habits; but the habits hold you still! Friend thus bound, to you I have to tell the glad news that Jesus Christ has come on purpose that he might proclaim the opening of the prisons to them that are bound. "He hath broken the gates of brass, and cut the bars of iron in sunder." God is able to liberate men from every bond of sin over which they mourn. Wouldst thou be free? He will open the door. There is no habit so inveterate, there is no passion so ferocious, but God can deliver you from it. If you will but trust in Jesus Christ, the Son of God, his grace is a hammer that can break your chains. Let Jesus say, "Loose him, and let him go," and not even devils can detain you. Christ's warrant runs over the whole universe; and, if he makes you free, you will be free indeed.

To advance another step, *these persons were weary men;* for we read of them, "he brought down their heart with labour." This does not happen to all in the same degree, but to some of us this labour was exceedingly grinding and exhausting. Our hearts were lofty, and needed bringing down; and the Lord used means to do it. With some, temporal circumstances go wrong: where everything used to prosper, everything appears to be under a blight. From abundance they descend to want. Perhaps the health also begins to give way, and from being strong and hearty men they become sickly and feeble. How often this tames proud spirits! If it be not outward sorrow, it is within that they labour till their heart is brought low. They cannot rest, and yet they try all earthly remedies for ease : they go to the theatre, they sport with gay companions, they laugh, they dance, they plunge into vice; but they cannot shake off the burden of their sin, it will not be removed. As the giraffe, when the lion has leaped upon him, bears his enemy upon his shoulders, and cannot dislodge him even though he rushes across the wilderness like the wind, so the sinner is being devoured by his sin while he madly labours to shake it off. While the unconverted seek to rest themselves, they do but increase their weariness. They labour, ay, labour as in the very fire ; but it is labour in vain. In vain do they hasten to every religious service, and attend to every sacred ceremony. In vain do they try to mourn; how can they put feeling into a heart of stone ? If they could, they would make their tears for ever flow, and their prayers for ever rise ; but, to their horror, they accomplish nothing. The whip of the law sounds, and they must get to their tasks again; but the more they do, the more they are undone. Like one that, having fallen into a slough, sinks all the deeper into the mire through every struggle that he makes, so do they fall lower and lower by their efforts to rise. I understand those awful strugglings of yours, so desperate and yet so unavailing. God is bringing down your heart with labour; but have you not had enough of this ? Do you not remember that love-word, "Come unto me, all ye that labour and are heavy-laden, and I will give you rest"? Sweet promise ; will you not believe it, and avail yourselves of it ? Will you not come to Jesus, and take the rest which he gives ? How I wish you would come this very day ! I beseech the Holy Spirit to turn you to Jesus. The Lord has come forth with power to draw you, and to bring you away from your weariness unto the sweet rest which remains for the people of God. Poor doves, fly no further ; return to your Noah ! These of whom we speak at this time were as weary men as ever *you* can be, but Jesus gave them rest; why should he not give rest to *you?* Though bad, and banned, and bound, and burdened, there is yet hope; for the Lord can set you free.

Again, *these persons were downcast men*—"they fell down, and there was none to help." "We cannot go on any longer," say they, "it is useless to exert ourselves. We cannot escape God's wrath, and yet we cannot bear it. We are at our wits' end. There is no use in our trying to be better. We must give it up in despair." "They fell down ;" this shows that they were quite spent. The captive has been grinding at the mill till he cannot go another round ; even the lash cannot make him take another step—he falls in faintness, as though life had gone. So have we known men forced to acknowledge that they are "without strength." This was always true, but they did not always feel it. Now they have come to this, that, if heaven could be had for one more effort, and hell escaped for one more good work, yet they could not do it. They fall down, and there they lie, a heap of helplessness, dead in trespasses and sins. Where is now the boasted power of their free-will ? Now it is to you who have fallen down, even to you, that the word of this salvation is sent. The Lord Jesus delights to lift up those that lie at his feet. He is a great overturner : " He hath put down the mighty from their seats, and exalted them of low degree." He that flies aloft on the eagle's wings of pride shall be brought low by the shafts of vengeance; but he that humbles himself to the dust shall be lifted up. He that has fallen down, and lies in the dust at the feet of Jesus, lies on the doorstep of eternal life. The Lord will give power to the weak, and increase strength to those who have no might. I rejoice when I hear any one of you own to his weakness, since the Lord Jesus will now show forth his power in you.

In fact, *these persons were helpless men:* "They fell down, and there was none to help." What a word that is—"None to help"! The proverb says, "God helps those that help themselves." There is a sort of truth in it; but I venture to cover it with a far greater truth: "God helps those that cannot help themselves." When there is none to help thee, then God will help thee. "There was none to help"—no priest, no minister, not even a praying wife, or a praying mother, could now do anything; the man felt that human helpers were of no avail. His bed was shorter than that he should stretch himself upon it, and his covering was narrower than that he should wrap himself up in it. Now he saw that there was no balm in Gilead, there was no physician there; and he looked to a higher place than Gilead for balm and medicine. The balm for such a wound as his must come from heaven, for on earth there was "none to help." This is a fitting epitaph to be placed over the grave of self-righteousness. This also is the death-knell of priest-craft, birthright membership, and sacramentarianism. The conscience sees that there is "none to help." Is this your case? Then you are the men in whom God will work the marvels of his grace, and bring you out where you shall walk in light and peace.

There was only one good point about these people—*they did at last take to praying:* "Then they cried unto the Lord in their trouble." It was not much of a prayer to hear; it was too shrill to be musical; it was too painful to be pleasant. "They cried," like one in sore anguish: they cried, like a child that has lost its mother; "they cried," like some poor wounded animal in great pain. Do you tell me that you cry, but that your cry is a very poor one? I know it, and I am glad to hear you say so, for the less you think of your cry the more God will think of it. Do you value yourself according to your prayers? Then your prayers have no value in them. When you think that your prayers are only broken words, and hideous moans, and wretched desires, then you begin to form a right estimate of them, and thus you are on true ground, where the Lord of truth can meet you. "They cried." Was it any credit to them to cry? Why, no, it was what they were forced to do! They would not have cried to the Lord even then if they could have done anything else. They cried when their hearts had been brought so low that they fell down. It is a good fall when a man falls on his knees. O my dear hearer, whatever else you do, or do not do, are you crying to God in secret for his grace? Then, as surely as the Lord liveth, you shall come out into liberty. A praying man shall never be sent to perdition. There is that about prayer which makes it a token for good, a pledge of blessings on the road, a door of hope in dark hours. Where is the man that cries? Where is the man that prays? That is the man of whom it shall be said, and of others like him, "The Lord brought them out of darkness and the shadow of death, and brake their bands in sunder."

May the Lord bless the description which I have given, so that some of you may see yourselves as in a looking-glass, and be encouraged to hope that the Lord will save you as he has saved others like you! If you do see yourself in the text, take home the comfort of it, and make use of it. Do not look at it, and say, "This belongs to somebody else." You bondaged brother, you self-despairing sinner, you are the man for whom Christ went up to the cross! If you saw a letter directed to yourself, would you not open it? I should think so. The other day a poor woman had a little help sent to her, by a friend, in a letter. She was in great distress, and she went to that very friend begging for a few shillings. "Why," said the other, "I sent you money yesterday, by an order in a letter!" "Dear, dear!" said the poor woman, "that must be the letter which I put behind the looking-glass!" Just so; and there are lots of people who put God's letters behind the looking-glass, and fail to make use of the promise which is meant for them. Come, all ye that labour and are heavy-laden, come and taste my Master's love, yea, take of it freely, and be filled with heavenly rest!

II. Secondly, may God's Spirit go with us while we answer the question: HOW HAS THIS DELIVERANCE BEEN WROUGHT? You that have been set free should tell how you were emancipated. Let me tell my story first. It was the gladdest news I ever heard when it was told me that Jesus died in my stead. I sat down in my misery, hopeless of salvation, ready to perish, till they told me that there was One who loved me, and for love of me was content to yield his life for my deliverance. Wonder of wonders, he had actually borne the death-penalty for me! They said that the Lord of glory had become man to save men, and that if I trusted him I might know assuredly that he had suffered in my stead, and so had blotted out my sins. I marvelled much as I heard this; but I felt that no one could have invented news so strange. It surpassed all fiction that the offended God should himself take my nature, and in the person of the Lord Jesus Christ should pay my debts, and suffer for my sins, and put those sins away. I heard the blessed tidings—there was some comfort even in hearing it—but I believed it, and clutched at it as for life. Then did I begin to live. I believe that truth to-day: all my hope lies there. If any of you wonder that I show fight for the substitutionary sacrifice of Christ, you may cease to wonder. Would not any one of you stand up for his wife and children? This truth is more to me than wife and children, it is everything to me. I am a damned man to all eternity if Christ did not die for me. I will put it no more softly than that. If my Redeemer has not borne my sins in his own body on the tree, then I shall have to bear them in my own body in the place of endless misery. I have no shade of a hope anywhere but in the sacrifice of Jesus; I cannot, therefore, give up this truth: I had sooner give up my life. I heard that the Son of God had suffered in my stead that I might go free: I believed it, and I said to myself, "Then I have no business to be sitting here in darkness and in the shadow of death." I shook myself from my lethargy, I arose, and went out of my prison; and as I moved to go out, a light shone round about me, and my fetters fell clanking to the ground. What glorious musical instruments they were! The very things that had galled me so long now brought me joy. I found that the iron gate, which I thought could never be unlocked, opened to me of its own accord. I could not believe that it was true, it seemed too wonderful; I thought I must be dreaming. I very soon knew of a surety that it was I myself. The cold night air blew down the street of my daily care, and I said, "Oh, yes, I am still on earth, and it is true, and I am free from despair, and delivered from the curse!" This is how I came out to liberty: I believed in Jesus my Redeemer. To-day, my dear brothers and sisters here, hundreds of them, would each one tell the story in a different way, but it would come to the same thing.

Follow me while we go a little into Scriptural detail, and learn from David how the Lord sets free the captives.

First, our deliverance was wrought *by the Lord himself*. Listen: "HE brought them out of darkness." Write that "HE" in capital letters, Mr. Printer. Have you in the house any specially large letters? If so, set up that word in the most prominent type you have:—"HE brought them out of darkness." Read also the sixteenth verse:—"HE hath broken the gates of brass." Did the Lord send an angel to liberate us? No; HE came himself in the person of his dear Son. When the Lord Jesus Christ had paid our enormous debt, did he leave us to accept our quittance entirely of our own free will, apart from his grace? Ah, no! the Holy Spirit came, and made us willing in the day of his power! "HE," "HE," "HE" wrought all the work *for* us, and all our works *in* us. "HE brought them out of darkness and the shadow of death." "Oh that men would praise the Lord, for HE hath broken the gates of brass." It is the Lord's doing; it is marvellous in our eyes. There is no salvation worth the having which has not the hand of the Godhead in it. It needs Father, Son, and Holy Ghost to save a soul. None but the Trinity can deliver a captive soul from the chains of sin and death and hell. Jehovah himself saves us.

Next, *the Lord did it alone*—"He hath broken the gates of brass." Nobody else was there to aid in liberating the prisoner. When our Lord Jesus trod the winepress, he was alone. When the Spirit of God came to work in us eternal life, he wrought alone. Instruments are condescendingly used to convey the word of life, but the life of the word is wholly of God. As to the divine Father, is it not true of "his own will begat he us by the word of truth"? He is the Author of our spiritual life, and he alone. None can share the work of our salvation with him, and none can divide the glory. Ho, you that are captives, are you looking for some man to help you? Remember, I pray you, that there is "none to help." "Salvation is of the Lord." Remember that verse, "Look unto me, and be ye saved, all the ends of the earth: for I am God, and there is none else;" that is to say, there is none else in the work of salvation except God. O soul, if thou hast to do with Christ Jesus, thou must have him at the beginning, thou must have him in the middle, thou must have him in the end, and thou must have him to fill up every nook and corner from the first to the last. He *alone* hath done it.

Note, too, that what he did was done *by the Lord's own goodness;* for the Psalmist says, "Oh that men would praise the Lord for his goodness!" His goodness took the form of mercy; as it is said in the first verse of this psalm, "O give thanks unto the Lord, for he is good : for his mercy endureth for ever ! " It must have been mercy, because those whom it blessed were as undeserving as they were miserable. They were guilty, guilty in action, and guilty in thought ; they had rebelled against the words of God, and contemned the counsel of the Most High ; yet he came, and set them free. You and I are always wanting to know before we give alms to beggars, "Are they deserving people ? " God gives the alms of his grace only to the undeserving. We respond to those who have a claim upon us ; God remembers those who have no claim whatever upon him. "Ah," says one, "but the people did cry ! " I know they did ; but they did not even do that till he first of all brought down their heart with labour. Prayer is a gift from God as well as an appeal to God. Even prayer for mercy is not a cause, but a result. Grace is at the back of prayer, and at the base of prayer. These prisoners would not have prayed if God had not wrought upon them, and driven and drawn them to pray.

> " No sinner can be
> Beforehand with thee ;
> Thy grace is most sovereign,
> Most rich, and most free."

So it has been with others, and therefore have I hope that it will be so with you, my beloved hearers. In the greatness of his goodness I trust my Lord will come and save you. It is not *your* goodness, but *his* goodness, which is the cause of hope : not your merit, but his mercy is his motive for blessing you. How greatly do I rejoice to remember that the Lord delighteth in mercy! It is his joy to pardon sin, and pass by the transgressions of the remnant of his people.

Note, once again, that while we are describing this great deliverance, we cannot help seeing that *the Lord effected it most completely.* What did he do ? Did he bring them out of darkness ? That was to give them *light.* Yes ; but a man that is chained is only a little better off for getting light, for then he can see his chains all the more. Notice what follows—"and out of the shadow of death": so the Lord gave them *life* as well as light. That "shadow of death" is gone, it can no longer brood over their darkened spirits. Yes, but when a man has light and life, if he is still in bondage, his life may make him feel his bondage the more vividly, and his light may make him long the more for liberty. But it is added, "and he brake their bands in sunder," which means *liberty.* The Lord gave light, life, and liberty—these three things. God does nothing by halves. He does not begin to save, and then say, "I have done enough for you. I must stop midway." Dear heart, if the Lord comes to your prison, he will not merely light a lamp in your dungeon, though that were something : he will not merely revive your spirit, and give you more life, though that were something ; but he will break your chains, and bring you out into the liberty wherewith Christ makes men free. He will finish his emancipating work. Do it, Lord; do it now! Help men to believe in Jesus at this moment !

There is one more point which I want you to notice very carefully. When the Lord does this, *he does this everlastingly.* He "brake their bands in sunder." When a man was set free from prison in the old times when they used iron chains, the smith came, and took the chains off, and then they were hung up upon the walls. Have you never been in ancient prisons, and seen the fetters and manacles hanging up ready for use; ay, for use upon those who have already worn such jewellery before, if they should come that way again? This is not the case here; for he "brake their bands in sunder." Note this right well, O child of God, you were once shut up as with gates of brass, and bars of iron, and the devil thinks that one of these days he will get you behind those gates again! But he never will, for the Lord "hath broken the gates of brass." All the powers of darkness cannot shut us up with broken gates! Satan thinks he will imprison us again; but the bars of iron are cut in sunder. The means of our captivity are no longer available. My mind carries me to a certain scene, and my eye almost beholds it. Behold Samson, the hero of Israel, shut in within the walls of Gaza. The Philistines boast, "Now will he be our captive." He slept till midnight, and then he arose. He found that he was shut up within the city, and so he went to the gate. That gate was barred and locked; but what mattered it? Israel's champion bowed his great shoulders down to the gate: he took hold of both the posts, gave a tremendous heave, and in an instant tore up the whole construction from the earth in which it had been firmly placed. "He lifted the doors of the gate of the city, and the two posts, and went away with them, and put them upon his shoulders, and carried them up to the top of a hill that is before Hebron." See in this thing a symbol of what our Lord Jesus Christ did when he arose from the dead. He carried away all that which held us captive—posts, and bar, and all. "He led captivity captive."

When our Lord had led us forth from our prison, he said to himself, "They shall never be shut up again, for now I will make sure work of it," and therefore he brake the gates of brass, and cut the bars of iron in sunder. How then can any child of God be shut up within the Gaza of sin again? How shall we be condemned when the Lord hath put away our sin for ever? No, the liberty received is everlasting liberty: we shall not see bondage any more. Oh, dear souls, I do want you to lay hold on this! You doomed and guilty men, you downcast and wearied men, there is everlasting salvation for you; not that which will save you to-day, and will let you go back to your bondage to-morrow; but that which will make you the Lord's free men for ever! If thou believest that Jesus is the Christ, if thou believest in him to save thee, thou shalt be saved. It is not said half-saved, but *saved*. "He that believeth and is baptized shall be saved." That cannot admit that we should go to hell. Jesus says, "I give unto my sheep eternal life; and they shall never perish, neither shall any man pluck them out of my hand." "He hath broken the gates of brass, and cut the bars of iron in sunder." Lord, help some poor souls to sing this song to-day, and receive at this moment everlasting salvation!

III. I close with a practical question: WHAT IS TO BE DONE ABOUT THIS? If such people as we have described have been brought into liberty, what is to be done about it? I do not want to tell you what to do, I would have you do it by instinct. Fain would I, like Miriam, take a timbrel, and go first, and bid all the sons and daughters of Israel follow me in this song : "Sing unto the Lord, for he hath triumphed gloriously. He hath brought out his captives. and set his people free." It naturally suggests itself to the liberated spirit to magnify the Lord. So the Psalmist put it, "Oh that men would praise the Lord for his goodness!"

First, then, if the Lord has set any of you free—*record it.* See how David wrote it down. Write it in your diary; write it so that friends may read it. Say, "The Lord hath done great things for us."

When you have recorded it, then *praise God.* Praise God with all your heart. Praise God every one of you. Praise God every day. When you have praised God yourselves, then entreat others to join with you. The oratorio of God's praise needs a full choir. I remember, years ago, a bill connected with a religious service of a very pretentious character, and on this bill it promised that the Hallelujah Chorus should be sung before the sermon. The friend who led the singing for me at that time came in to me, and asked if I could spare him. "See here," said he, "a person has come from the service which has been advertised to say that they have nobody to sing the Hallelujah Chorus. The minister wants me to go down and do it." I answered, "Yes; by all means go. If you can sing the Hallelujah Chorus alone, don't throw yourself away on me." Then we smiled, and at last broke out into a laugh; it was too much for our gravity. Surely for a man to think that he can sufficiently praise God alone is much like attempting to sing the Hallelujah Chorus as a solo. The Psalmist therefore utters that great "Oh!" "Oh that men would praise the Lord!" I do not think he said "men," for the word "men" is in italics: the translators are accountable for it. He means: Oh that angels, oh that cherubim and seraphim would praise the Lord! Oh that all creatures that have breath would praise the Lord for his goodness! Even that would not be enough, but let the mountains and the hills break forth before him into singing, and let all the trees of the wood clap their hands. Let the sea roar and the fulness thereof, the world and they that dwell therein. With a great "Oh!" with a mighty sigh over the holy business, which was far too great for himself, David felt moved to call upon all others to praise the Lord.

I close with that; my brothers, my sisters, you that have been saved, praise God! Praise him with the blessings he has lavished on you. I described them in three ways. With your *light* praise him : the more you know, the more you see, the more you understand, turn it all into praise. Next, with your *life* praise him—with your physical life, with your mental life, with your spiritual life : with life of every sort even unto eternal life praise the Lord. *Liberty* has been given us; let our freedom praise him. Be like that man who was made straight, who went out of the temple, walking, and leaping, and praising God. God has made you free, feel free to praise him : and if men will not give you leave to praise, take French leave ; yea, take heavenly leave, and praise God anywhere and everywhere. Hark! how they sing the songs of Bacchus and of Venus in the streets, and even wake us up in the night: why may not we sing God's praises in the same public fashion? We must praise him! We will praise him! We do praise him! We shall praise him for ever and ever!

Praise him with the heart he has changed, with the lips he has loosed, with the lives he has spared. A little while ago you could not speak a cheerful word, but now you can rejoice in God. Let those lips, from which he has taken the muzzle of dumb despair, be opened in his praise. Praise him with all the talents he has lent you. If you have any power of thought, if you have any fluency of speech, praise him. If you have any voice of song, praise him. If you have health and strength, praise him. Let every limb of your body praise him: those members which were servants of sin, let them be instruments of righteousness unto God. Praise him with your substance. Let your gold and silver, ay, and your bronze, praise him. Praise him with all that you have, and with all that you are, and with all that you hope to be. Lay your all upon the altar. Make a whole burnt-offering of it. Praise him with all the influence you have. If he has delivered you from the shadow of death, let your shadow, like that of Peter, become the instrument of God's healing power to others. Teach others to praise God. Influence them by your example. Fill your house with music from top to bottom; perfume every room with the fragrance of living devotion. Make your houses belfries, and be yourselves the bells for ever ringing out the loud praises of the Lamb of God. He bore your sins, bear you his praises. He died for you, therefore live for him. He has heard your prayers, let him hear your praises. Let us together sing "Hallelujah to God and the Lamb." Let us stand upon our feet, and with one voice and heart let us sing:

> " Praise God, from whom all blessings flow,
> Praise him all creatures here below,
> Praise him above, ye heavenly host,
> Praise Father, Son, and Holy Ghost."

Young Man,

Is This for You?

"And it came to pass the day after, that he went into a city called Nain ; and many of his disciples went with him, and much people. Now when he came nigh to the gate of the city, behold, there was a dead man carried out, the only son of his mother, and she was a widow : and much people of the city was with her. And when the Lord saw her, he had compassion on her, and said unto her, Weep not. And he came and touched the bier : and they that bare him stood still. And he said, Young man, I say unto thee, Arise. And he that was dead sat up, and began to speak. And he delivered him to his mother. And there came a fear on all : and they glorified God, saying, That a great prophet is risen up among us ; and, That God hath visited his people. And this rumour of him went forth throughout all Judæa, and throughout all the region round about."—Luke vii. 11—17.

BEHOLD, dear brethren, the overflowing, ever-flowing power of our Lord Jesus Christ. He had wrought a great work upon the centurion's servant, and now, only a day after, he raises the dead. "It came to pass the day after, that he went into a city called Nain." Day unto day uttereth speech concerning his deeds of goodness. Did he save your friend yesterday ? His fulness is the same ; if you seek him, his love and grace will flow to you to-day. He blesses this day, and he blesses the day after. Never is our divine Lord compelled to pause until he has recruited his resources ; but virtue goeth out of him for ever. These thousands of years have not diminished the aboundings of his power to bless.

Behold, also, the readiness and naturalness of the outgoings of his life-giving power. Our Saviour was journeying, and he works miracles while on the road : "He went into a city called Nain." It was incidentally, some would say accidentally, that he met the funeral procession ; but at once he restored to life this dead young man. Our blessed Lord was not standing still, as one professionally called in ; he does not seem to have come to Nain at any one's request for the display of his love ; but he was passing through the gate into the city, for some reason which is not recorded. See, my brethren, how the Lord Jesus is always ready to save ! He healed the woman who touched him in the throng when he was on the road to quite another person's house. The mere spillings and droppings of the Lord's cup of grace are marvellous. Here he gives life to the dead when he is *en route ;* he scatters his mercy by the roadside, and anywhere and everywhere his paths drop fatness. No time, no place, can find Jesus unwilling or unable. When Baal is on a journey, or sleepeth, his deluded worshippers cannot hope for his help; but when Jesus journeys or sleeps, a word will find him ready to conquer death, or quell the tempest.

It was a remarkable incident, this meeting of the two processions at the gates of Nain. If some one with a fine imagination could picture it, what an opportunity he would have for developing his poetical genius! I venture on no such effort. Yonder a procession descends from the city. Our spiritual eyes see death upon the pale horse coming forth from the city gate with great exultation. He has taken another captive. Upon that bier behold the spoils of the dread conqueror! Mourners by their tears confess the victory of death. Like a general riding in triumph to the Roman capitol, death bears his spoils to the tomb. What shall hinder him? Suddenly the procession is arrested by another: a company of disciples and much people are coming up the hill. We need not look at the company, but we may fix our eyes upon one who stands in the centre, a man in whom lowliness was always evident, and yet majesty was never wanting. It is the living Lord, even he who only hath immortality, and in him death has now met his destroyer. The battle is short and decisive; no blows are struck, for death has already done his utmost. With a finger the chariot of death is arrested; with a word the spoil is taken from the mighty, and the lawful captive is delivered. Death flies defeated from the gates of the city, while Tabor and Hermon, which both looked down upon the scene, rejoice in the name of the Lord. This was a rehearsal upon a small scale of that which shall happen by-and-by, when those who are in their graves shall hear the voice of the Son of God and live: then shall the last enemy be destroyed. Only let death come into contact with him who is our life, and it is compelled to relax its hold, whatever may be the spoil which it has captured. Soon shall our Lord come in his glory, and then before the gates of the New Jerusalem we shall see the miracle at the gates of Nain multiplied a myriad times.

Thus, you see, our subject would naturally conduct us to the doctrine of the resurrection of the dead, which is one of the foundation stones of our most holy faith. That grand truth I have often declared to you, and will do so again and again; but at this time I have selected my text for a very practical purpose, which concerns the souls of some for whom I am greatly anxious. The narrative before us records a fact, a literal fact, but the record may be used for spiritual instruction. All our Lord's miracles were intended to be parables: they were intended to instruct as well as to impress : they are sermons to the eye, just as his spoken discourses were sermons to the ear. We see here how Jesus can deal with spiritual death; and how he can impart spiritual life at his pleasure. Oh, that we may see this done this morning in the midst of this great assembly !

I. I shall ask you first, dear friends, to reflect that THE SPIRITUALLY DEAD CAUSE GREAT GRIEF TO THEIR GRACIOUS FRIENDS. If an ungodly man is favoured to have Christian relatives, he causes them much anxiety. As a natural fact, this dead young man, who was being carried out to his burial, caused his mother's heart to burst with grief. She showed by her tears that her heart was overflowing with sorrow. The Saviour said to her, "Weep not," because he saw how deeply she was troubled. Many of my dear young friends may be deeply thankful that they have friends who are grieving over them. It is a sad thing that your conduct should grieve them; but it is a hopeful circumstance for you that you have those around you who do thus grieve. If all approved of your evil ways, you would, no doubt, continue in them, and go speedily to destruction; but it is a blessing that arresting voices do at least a little hinder you. Besides, it may yet be that our Lord will listen to the silent oratory of your mother's tears, and that this morning he may bless you for her sake. See how the evangelist puts it: "When the Lord saw *her*, he had compassion on *her*, and said unto *her*, Weep not." And then he said to the young man, "Arise."

Many young persons who are in some respects amiable and hopeful, nevertheless, being spiritually dead, *are causing great sorrow to those who love them best*. It would perhaps be honest to say that they do not intend to inflict all this sorrow; indeed, they think it quite unnecessary. Yet they are a daily burden to those whom they love. Their conduct is such that when it is thought over in the silence of their mother's chamber, she cannot help but weep. Her son went with her to the house of God when he was a boy, but now he finds his pleasure in a very different quarter. Being beyond all control now, the young man does not choose to go with his mother. She would not wish to deprive him of his liberty, but she laments that he exercises that liberty so unwisely; she mourns that he has not the inclination to hear the Word of the Lord, and become a servant of his mother's God. She had hoped that he would follow in his father's footsteps, and unite with the people of God; but he takes quite the opposite course. She has seen a good deal about him lately which has deepened her anxiety: he is forming companionships and other connections which are sadly harmful to him. He has a distaste for the quietude of home, and he has been exhibiting to his mother a spirit which wounds her. It may be that what he has said and done is not meant to be unkind; but it is very grievous to the heart which watches over him so tenderly. She sees a growing indifference to everything that is good, and an unconcealed intention to see the vicious side of life. She knows a little, and fears more, as to his present state, and she dreads that he will go from one sin to another till he ruins himself for this life and the next. O friends, it is to a gracious heart a very great grief to have an unconverted child; and yet more so if that child is a mother's boy, her only boy, and she a desolate woman, from whom her husband has been snatched away. To see spiritual death rampant in one so dear is a sore sorrow, which causes many a mother to mourn in secret, and pour out her soul before God. Many a Hannah has become a woman of a sorrowful spirit through her own child. How sad that he who should have made her the gladdest among women has filled her life with bitterness! Many a mother has had so to grieve over her son as almost to cry, "Would God he had never been born!" It is so in thousands of cases. If it be so in your case, dear friend, take home my words to yourself, and reflect upon them.

The cause of grief lies here : *we mourn that they should be in such a case*. In the story before us the mother wept because her son was dead; and we sorrow because our young friends are spiritually dead. There is a life infinitely higher than the life which quickens our material bodies; and oh that all of you knew it! You, who are unrenewed, do not know anything about this true life. Oh, how we wish you did! It seems to us a dreadful thing that you should be dead to God, dead to Christ, dead to the Holy Spirit. It is sad, indeed, that you should be dead to those divine truths which are the delight and strength of our souls; dead to those holy motives which keep us back from evil, and spur us on to virtue; dead to those sacred joys which often bring us very near the gates of heaven. We cannot look at a dead man, and feel joy in him, whoever he may be : a corpse, however delicately dressed, is a sad sight. We cannot look upon you, ye poor dead souls, without crying out, " O God, shall it always be so? Shall not these dry bones live? Wilt thou not quicken them?" The apostle speaks of one who lived in pleasure, and he said of her, " She is dead while she liveth." Numbers of persons are dead in reference to all that is truest, and noblest, and most divine; and yet in other respects they are full of life and activity. Oh, to think that they should be dead to God, and yet so full of jollity and energy! Marvel not that we grieve about them.

We also mourn because we lose the help and comfort which they ought to bring us. This widowed mother no doubt mourned her boy, not only because he was dead, but because in him she had lost her earthly stay. She must have regarded him as the staff of her age, and the comfort of her loneliness. " She was a widow ": I question if anybody but a widow understands the full sorrow of that word. We may put ourselves by sympathy into the position of one who has lost her other self, the partner of her life; but the tenderest sympathy cannot fully realize the actual cleavage of bereavement, and the desolation of love's loss. " She was a widow "—the sentence sounds like a knell. Still, if the sun of her life was gone, there was a star shining; she had a boy, a dear boy, who promised her great comfort. He would, no doubt, supply her necessities, and cheer her loneliness, and in him her husband would live again, and his name would remain among the living in Israel. She could lean on him as she went to the synagogue; she would have him to come home from his work at evening, and keep the little home together, and cheer her hearth. Alas! that star is swallowed up in the darkness. He is dead, and to-day he is borne to the cemetery. It is the same spiritually with us in reference to our unconverted friends. With regard to you that are dead in sin, we feel that we miss the aid and comfort which we ought to receive from you in our service of the living God. We want fresh labourers in all sorts of places—in our Sunday-school work, our mission among the masses, and in all manner of service for the Lord we love! Ours is a gigantic burden, and we long for our sons to put their shoulders to it. We did look forward to see you grow up in the fear of God, and stand side by side with us in the great warfare against evil, and in holy labour for the Lord Jesus; but you cannot help us, for you are yourselves on the wrong side. Alas, alas! you hinder us by causing the world to say, "See how those young men are acting!" We have to spend thought, and prayer, and effort over you which might usefully have gone forth for others. Our care for yonder great dark world which lies all around us is very pressing, but you do not share it with us: men are perishing from lack of knowledge, and you do not help us in endeavouring to enlighten them.

A further grief is that we can have no fellowship with them. The mother at Nain could have no communion with her dear son now that he was dead, for the dead know not anything. He can never speak to her, nor she to him, for he is on the bier, "a dead man carried out." O my friends, certain of you have dear ones whom you love, and they love you; but they cannot hold any spiritual communion with you, nor you with them. You never bow the knee together in private prayer, nor mingle heart with heart in the appeal of faith to God as to the cares which prowl around your home. O young man, when your mother's heart leaps for joy because of the love of Christ shed abroad in her soul, you cannot understand her joy. Her feelings are a mystery to you. If you are a dutiful son, you do not say anything disrespectful about her religion; but yet you cannot sympathize in its sorrows or its joys. Between your mother and you there is upon the best things a gulf as wide as if you were actually dead on the bier, and she stood weeping over your corpse. I remember, in the hour of overwhelming anguish when I feared that my beloved wife was about to be taken from me, how I was comforted by the loving prayers of my two dear sons: we had communion not only in our grief, but in our confidence in the living God. We knelt together and poured out our hearts unto God, and we were comforted. How I blessed God that I had in my children such sweet support! But suppose they had been ungodly young men! I should have looked in vain for holy fellowship, and for aid at the throne of grace. Alas! in many a household the mother cannot have communion with her own son or daughter on that point which is most vital and enduring, because they are spiritually dead, while she has been quickened into newness of life by the Holy Spirit.

Moreover, *spiritual death soon produces manifest causes for sorrow.* In the narrative before us the time had come when her son's body must be buried. She could not wish to have that dead form longer in the home with her. It is a token to us of the terrible power of death, that it conquers love with regard to the body. Abraham loved his Sarah; but after a while he had to say to the sons of Heth, "Give me a possession of a burying-place with you, that I may bury my dead out of my sight." It happens in some mournful cases that character becomes so bad that no comfort in life can be enjoyed while the erring one is within the home circle. We have known parents who have felt that they could not have their son at home, so drunken, so debauched had he become. Not always wisely, yet sometimes almost of necessity, the plan has been tried of sending the incorrigible youth to a distant colony, in the hope that when removed from pernicious influences he might do better. How seldom so deplorable an experiment succeeds! I have known mothers who could not think of their sons without feeling pangs far more bitter than those they endured at their birth. Woe, woe to him who causes such heart-break!

What an awful thing it is when love's best hopes gradually die down into despair, and loving desires at last put on mourning, and turn from prayers of hope to tears of regret! Words of admonition call forth such passion and blasphemy that prudence almost silences them. Then have we before us the dead young man carried out to his grave. A sorrowful voice sobs out, "He is given unto idols, let him alone." Am I addressing one whose life is now preying upon the tender heart of her that brought him forth? Do I speak to one whose outward conduct has at last become so avowedly wicked that he is a daily death to those who gave him life? O young man, can you bear to think of this? Are you turned to stone? I cannot yet believe that you contemplate your parents' heart-break without bitter feelings. God forbid that you should!

We also mourn because of the future of men dead in sin. This mother, whose son had already gone so far in death that he must be buried out of sight, had the further knowledge that something worse would befall him in the sepulchre to which he was being carried. It was impossible for her to think calmly of the corruption which surely follows at the heels of death. When we think of what will become of you who refuse the Lord Christ we are appalled. "After death the judgment." We could more readily go into details as to a putrid corpse than we could survey the state of a soul lost for ever. We dare not linger at the mouth of hell; but we are forced to remind you that there is a place "where their worm dieth not, and the fire is not quenched." There is a place where those must abide who are driven from the presence of the Lord, and from the glory of his power. It is an unendurable thought, that you should be "cast into the lake of fire, which is the second death." I do not wonder that those who are not honest with you are afraid to tell you so, and that you try yourself to doubt it; but with the Bible in your hand, and a conscience in your bosom, you cannot but fear the worst if you remain apart from Jesus and the life he freely gives. If you continue as you are, and persevere in your sin and unbelief to the end of life, there is no help for it but that you must be condemned in the day of judgment. The most solemn declarations of the Word of God assure you that "he that believeth not shall be damned." It is heart-breaking work to think that this should be the case with any one of you. You prattled at your mother's knee, and kissed her cheek with rapturous love; why, then, will you be divided from her for ever? Your father hoped that you would take his place in the church of God; how is it that you do not even care to follow him to heaven? Remember, the day comes when "one shall be taken, and the other left." Do you renounce all hope of being with your wife, your sister, your mother, at the right hand of God? You cannot wish them to go down to hell with you; have you no desire to go to heaven with them? "Come, ye blessed," will be the voice of Jesus to those who imitated their gracious Saviour; and "Depart from me, ye cursed, into everlasting fire, prepared for the devil and his angels," must be the sentence upon all who refuse to be made like the Lord. Why will you take your part and lot with accursed ones?

I do not know whether you find it easy to hear me this morning.

I find it very hard to speak to you, because my lips are not able to express my heart's feelings. Oh that I had the forceful utterance of an Isaiah, or the passionate lamentations of a Jeremiah, with which to arouse your affections and your fears! Still, the Holy Spirit can use even me, and I beseech him so to do. It is enough. I am sure you see that the spiritually dead cause great grief to those of their family who are spiritually alive.

II. Now let me cheer you while I introduce the second head of my discourse, which is this: FOR SUCH GRIEF THERE IS ONLY ONE HELPER: BUT THERE IS A HELPER. This young man is taken out to be buried; but *our Lord Jesus Christ met the funeral procession.* Carefully note the " coincidences," as sceptics call them, but as we call them " providences " of Scripture." This is a fine subject for another time. Take this one case. How came it that the young man died just then? How came it that this exact hour was selected for his burial? Perhaps because it was evening; but even that might not fix the precise moment. Why did the Saviour that day arrange to travel five-and-twenty miles, so as to arrive at Nain in the evening? How came it to pass that he happened just then to be coming from a quarter which naturally led him to enter at that particular gate from which the dead would be borne? See, he ascends the hill to the little city at the same moment when the head of the procession is coming out of the gate! He meets the dead man before the place of sepulture is reached. A little later and he would have been buried; a little earlier and he would have been at home lying in the darkened room, and no one might have called the Lord's attention to him. The Lord knows how to arrange all things; his forecasts are true to the tick of the clock. I hope some great purpose is to be fulfilled this morning. I do not know why you, my friend, came in here on a day when I am discoursing on this particular subject. You did not think to come, perhaps, but here you are. And Jesus has come here too; he has come here on purpose to meet you, and quicken you to newness of life. There is no chance about it, eternal decrees have arranged it all, and we shall soon see that it is so. You being spiritually dead are met by him in whom is life eternal.

The blessed Saviour saw all at a glance. Out of that procession he singled out the chief mourner, and read her inmost heart. He was always tender to mothers. He fixed his eye on that widow; for he knew that she was such, without being informed of the fact. The dead man is her only son: he perceives all the details, and feels them all intensely. O young man, Jesus knows all about you. Nothing is hid from his infinite mind. Your mother's heart and yours are both open to him. Jesus, who is invisibly present this morning, fixes his eyes on you at this moment. He has seen the tears of those who have wept for you. He sees that some of them despair of you, and are in their great grief acting like mourners at your funeral.

Jesus saw it all, and, what was more, *entered into it all.* Oh, how we ought to love our Lord that he takes such notice of our griefs, and especially our spiritual griefs about the souls of others! You, dear teacher, want your class saved: Jesus sympathizes with you. You, dear friend, have been very earnest to win souls. Know that in all this you are workers together with God. Jesus knows all about our travail of soul, and he is at one with us therein. Our travail is only his own travail rehearsed in us, according to our humble measure. When Jesus enters into our work it cannot fail. Enter, O Lord, into my work at this hour, I pray thee, and bless this feeble word to my hearers! I know that hundreds of believers are saying, "Amen." How this cheers me!

Our Lord proved how he entered into the sorrowful state of things by first saying to the widow, "Weep not." At this moment he says to you who are praying and agonizing for souls, "Do not despair! Sorrow not as those who are without hope! I mean to bless you. You shall yet rejoice over life given to the dead." Let us take heart and dismiss all unbelieving fear.

Our Lord then went to the bier, and just laid his finger upon it, and *they that bare it stood still of their own accord.* Our Lord has a way of making bearers stand still without a word. Perhaps to-day yonder young man is being carried further into sin by the four bearers of his natural passions, his infidelity, his bad company, and his love of strong drink. It may be that pleasure and pride, wilfulness and wickedness are bearing the four corners of the bier; but our Lord can, by his mysterious power, make the bearers stand still. Evil influences have become powerless, the man knows not how.

When they stood quite still, *there was a hush.* The disciples stood around the Lord, the mourners surrounded the widow, and the two crowds faced each other. There was a little space, and Jesus and the dead man were in the centre. The widow pushed away her veil, and gazing through her tears wondered what was coming. The Jews who came out of the city halted as the bearers had done. Hush! Hush! What will HE do? In that deep silence the Lord heard the unspoken prayers of that widow woman. I doubt not that her soul began to whisper, half in hope, and half in fear—"Oh, that he would raise my son!" At any rate, Jesus heard the flutter of the wings of desire if not of faith. Surely her eyes were speaking as she gazed on Jesus, who had so suddenly appeared. Here let us be as quiet as the scene before us. Let us be hushed for a minute, and pray God to raise dead souls at this time. (Here followed a pause, much silent prayer, and many tears.)

III. That hush was not long, for speedily the Great Quickener entered upon his gracious work. This is our third point: JESUS IS ABLE TO WORK THE MIRACLE OF LIFE-GIVING. Jesus Christ has life in himself, and he quickeneth whom he will (John v. 21). Such life is there in him that "he that liveth and believeth in him, though he were dead, yet shall he live." Our blessed Lord immediately went up to the bier. What lay before him? It was a corpse. *He could derive no aid from that lifeless form.* The spectators were sure that he was dead, for they were carrying him out to bury him. No deception was possible, for his own mother believed him dead, and you may be sure that if there had been a spark of life in him she would not have given him up to the jaws of the grave. There was then no hope—no hope from the dead man, no hope from any one in the crowd either of bearers or of disciples. They were all powerless alike. Even so, you, O sinner, cannot save yourself, neither can any of us, or all of us save you.

There is no help for you, dead sinner, beneath yon skies; no help in yourself or in those who love you best. But, lo, the Lord hath laid help on one that is mighty. If Jesus wants the least help you cannot render it, for you are dead in sins. There you lie, dead on the bier, and nothing but the sovereign power of divine omnipotence can put heavenly life into you. Your help must come from above.

While the bier stood still, Jesus spoke to the dead young man, *spoke to him personally:* "Young man, I say unto thee, Arise." O Master, personally speak to some young man this morning; or, if thou wilt, speak to the old, or speak to a woman; but speak the word home to them. We mind not where the Lord's voice may fall. Oh that it would now call those around me, for I feel that there are dead ones all over the building! I stand with biers all about me, and dead ones on them. Lord Jesus, art thou not here? What is wanted is thy personal call. Speak, Lord, we beseech thee!

"Young man," said he, "arise;" and *he spake as if the man had been alive.* This is the gospel way. He did not wait till he saw signs of life before he bade him rise; but to the dead man he said, "Arise." This is the model of gospel preaching: in the name of the Lord Jesus, his commissioned servants speak to the dead as if they were alive. Some of my brethren cavil at this, and say that it is inconsistent and foolish; but all through the New Testament it is even so. There we read, "Arise from the dead, and Christ shall give thee light." I do not attempt to justify it; it is more than enough for me that so I read the Word of God. We are to bid men believe on the Lord Jesus Christ, even though we know that they are dead in sin, and that faith is the work of the Spirit of God. Our faith enables us in God's name to command dead men to live, and they do live. We bid unbelieving man believe in Jesus, and power goes with the Word, and God's elect do believe. It is by this word of faith which we preach that the voice of Jesus sounds out to men. The young man who could not rise, for he was dead, nevertheless did rise when Jesus bade him. Even so, when the Lord speaks by his servants the gospel command, "Believe and live," is obeyed, and men live.

But the Saviour, you observe, *spoke with his own authority*—"Young man, *I say unto thee*, Arise." Neither Elijah nor Elisha could thus have spoken; but he who spoke thus was very God of very God. Though veiled in human flesh, and clothed in lowliness, he was that same God who said, "Let there be light, and there was light." If any of us are able by faith to say, "Young man, Arise," we can only say it in *his* name—we have no authority but what we derive from *him*. Young man, the voice of Jesus can do what your mother cannot. How often has her sweet voice wooed you to come to Jesus, but wooed in vain! Oh, that the Lord Jesus would inwardly speak to you! Oh, that he would say, "Young man, Arise." I trust that while I am speaking the Lord is silently speaking in your hearts by his Holy Spirit. I feel sure that it is even so. If so, within you a gentle movement of the Spirit is inclining you to repent and yield your heart to Jesus. This shall be a blessed day to the spiritually dead young man, if now he accepts his Saviour, and yields himself up to be renewed by grace. No, my poor brother, they shall not bury you! I know you have been very bad, and they may well despair of you; but while Jesus lives we cannot give you up.

The miracle was wrought straightway : for this young man, to the astonishment of all about him, sat up. His was a desperate case, but death was conquered, for he sat up. He had been called back from the innermost dungeon of death, even from the grave's mouth; but he sat up when Jesus called him. It did not take a month, nor a week, nor an hour, nay, not even five minutes. Jesus said, "Young man, Arise." And he that was dead sat up, and began to speak." In an instant the Lord can save a sinner. Ere the words I speak can have more than entered your ear, the divine flash which gives you eternal life can have penetrated your breast, and you shall be a new creature in Jesus Christ, beginning to live in newness of life from this hour, no more to feel spiritually dead, or to return to your old corruption. New life, new feeling, new love, new hopes, new company shall be yours, because you have passed from death unto life. Pray God that it may be so, for he will hear us.

IV. Our time has gone, and although we have a wide subject we may not linger. I must close by noticing that THIS WILL PRODUCE VERY GREAT RESULTS. To give life to the dead is no little matter.

The great result was manifest, first, in the young man. Would you like to see him as he was? Might I venture to draw back the sheet from his face? See there what death has done. He was a fine young man. To his mother's eye he was the mirror of manhood! What a pallor is on that face! How sunken are the eyes! You are feeling sad. I see you cannot bear the sight. Come, look into this grave, where corruption has gone further in its work. Cover him up! We cannot bear to look at the decaying body! But when Jesus Christ has said, "Arise," what a change takes place! Now you may look at him. His blue eye has the light of heaven in it; his lips are coral red with life; his brow is fair and full of thought. Look at his healthy complexion, in which the rose and the lily sweetly contend for mastery. What a fresh look there is about him, as of the dew of the morning! He has been dead, but he lives, and no trace of death is on him. While you are looking at him he begins to speak. What music for his mother's ear! What did he say? Why, that I cannot tell you. Speak yourself as a newly-quickened one, and then I shall hear what you say. I know what *I* said. I think the first word I said when I was quickened was, "Hallelujah." Afterwards, I went home to my mother, and told her that the Lord had met with me. No words are given here. It does not quite matter what those words are, for any words proved him to be alive. If you know the Lord, I believe you will speak of heavenly things. I do not believe that our Lord Jesus has a dumb child in his house: they all speak *to* him, and most of them speak *of* him. The new birth reveals itself in confession of Christ, and praise of Christ. I warrant you, that his mother, when she heard him speak, did not criticize what he said. She did not say, "That sentence is ungrammatical." She was too glad to hear him speak at all, that she did not examine all the expressions which he used. Newly-saved souls often talk in a way which after years and experience will not justify. You often hear it said of a revival meeting, that there was a good deal of excitement, and certain young converts talked absurdly. That is very likely : but if genuine grace was in their souls, and they bore witness to the Lord Jesus, I for one would not criticize them very severely. Be glad if you can see any proof that they are born again, and mark well their future lives. To the young man himself a new life had begun—life from among the dead.

A new life also had begun in reference to *his mother*. What a great result for her was the raising of her dead son ! Henceforth he would be doubly dear. Jesus helped him down from the bier, and delivered him to his mother. We have not the words he used; but we are sure that he made the presentation most gracefully, giving back the son to the mother as one presents a choice gift. With a majestic delight which always goes with his condescending benevolence, he looked on that happy woman, and his glance was brighter to her than the light of the morning, as he said to her, "Receive thy son." The thrill of her heart was such as she would never forget. Observe carefully that our Lord, when he puts the new life into young men, does not want to take them away with him from the home where their first duty lies. Here and there one is called away to be an apostle or a missionary; but usually he wants them to go home to their friends, and bless their parents, and make their families happy and holy. He does not present the young man to the priest, but he delivers him to his mother. Do not say, "I am converted, and therefore I cannot go to business any more, or try to support my mother by my trade." That would prove that you were not converted at all. You may go for a missionary in a year or two's time if you are fitted for it; but you must not make a dash at a matter for which you are not prepared. For the present go home to your mother, and make your home happy, and charm your father's heart, and be a blessing to your brothers and sisters, and let them rejoice because "he was dead, and is alive again; he was lost, and is found."

What was the next result? Well, all the neighbours feared and glorified God. If yonder young man who last night was at the music-hall, and a few nights ago came home very nearly drunk; if that young man is born again, all around him will wonder at it. If that young man who has got himself out of a situation by gambling, or some other wrong-doing, is saved, we shall all feel that God is very near us. If that young man who has begun to associate with evil women, and to fall into other evils, is brought to be pure-minded and gracious, it will strike awe into those round about him. He has led many others astray, and if the Lord now leads him back it will make a great hubbub, and men will enquire as to the reason of the change, and will see that there is a power in religion after all. Conversions are miracles which never cease. These prodigies of power in the moral world are quite as remarkable as prodigies in the material world. We want conversion, so practical, so real, so divine, that those who doubt will not be able to doubt, because they see in them the hand of God.

Finally, note that it not only surprised the neighbours and impressed them, but the rumour of it went everywhere. Who can tell? If a convert is made this morning, the result of that conversion may be felt for thousands of years, if the world stands so long; ay, it shall be felt when a thousand thousand years have passed away, even throughout eternity. Tremblingly have I dropped a smooth stone into the lake this morning. It has fallen from a feeble hand and from an earnest heart. Your tears have shown that the waters are stirred. I perceive the first circlet upon the surface. Other and wider circles will follow as the sermon is spoken of and read. When you go home and tell what God has done for your soul, there will be a wider ring; and if it should happen that the Lord should open the mouth of one of this morning's converts to preach his word, then no one can tell how wide the circle will become. Ring upon ring will the word spread itself, until the shoreless ocean of eternity shall feel the influence of this morning's word. No, I am not dreaming. According to our faith so shall it be. Grace this day bestowed by the Lord upon one single soul may affect the whole mass of humanity. God grant his blessing, even life for evermore. Pray much for a blessing. My dear friends, I beseech you, for Jesus Christ's sake, pray much for me. Amen.

The Maintenance
of Good Works

"For we ourselves also were sometimes foolish, disobedient, deceived, serving divers lusts and pleasures, living in malice and envy, hateful, and hating one another. But after that the kindness and love of God our Saviour toward man appeared, not by works of righteousness which we have done, but according to his mercy he saved us, by the washing of regeneration, and renewing of the Holy Ghost; which he shed on us abundantly through Jesus Christ our Saviour; that being justified by his grace, we should be made heirs according to the hope of eternal life. This is a faithful saying, and these things I will that thou affirm constantly, that they which have believed in God might be careful to maintain good works. These things are good and profitable unto men."—Titus iii. 3—8.

LAST Thursday evening my sermon was based upon the contrast, in the second chapter of Ephesians, between the expressions "not of works" and "created in Christ Jesus unto good works." I tried to show the true place of good works in connection with salvation. Many of you were not present then, and I felt that the subject was of such extreme importance that I must return to the same line of thought in this greater congregation. I shall endeavour by another text, which contains the same contrast, to set before you the usefulness, the benefit, yea, and the absolute necessity for our abounding in good works, if indeed we are saved by faith in Christ Jesus.

Let us come at once to our text. Our apostle tells us that we are to speak evil of no man, but to show meekness unto all men; and he adds this as an all-sufficient reason—we ourselves also were sometimes like the very worst of them. When we look upon the world at this day, it pains us by its folly, disobedience, and delusion. He that knows most of this modern Babylon, whether he observes the richer or the poorer classes of society, will find the deepest cause for grief. But we cannot condemn with bitterness, for such were some of us. Not only can we not condemn with bitterness, but we look upon our sinful fellow-creatures with great compassion, for such were some of us. Yea more, we feel encouraged to hope for ungodly men, even for the foolish and disobedient, for we ourselves also were, not long ago, like them. We feel that we must give the thought of our heart and the energy of our lives to the great work of saving men, out of gratitude to the Lord our God, who, in his kindness and love, has saved us. "I am a man," said one, "and everything that has to do with

91

men concerns me ": but the child of God adds to this, " I am also a sinful man, and owe my cleansing to the loving favour of the Lord. I was in the same mire of sin as these are in ; and if I am now washed in the laver of regeneration, and renewed by the Holy Ghost, I owe it all to sovereign grace, and am bound by love to man and love to God to seek the cleansing and renewal of my fellow-men." Eyes that have wept over our own sin will always be most ready to weep over the sins of others. If you have judged yourselves with candour, you will not judge others with severity. You will be more ready to pity than to condemn, more anxious to hide a multitude of sins than to punish a single sinner. I will give little for your supposed regeneration if there is not created in you a tender heart, which can truly say—

> " My God, I feel the mournful scene ;
> My bowels yearn o'er dying men ;
> And fain my pity would reclaim,
> And snatch the firebrands from the flame."

With this feeling towards mankind at large, we are led to consider the divine remedy for sinfulness, and to look with pleasure upon what God has devised for the creation of holiness in a fallen race. He at first created man a pure and spotless being. When he placed Adam in the garden, he made a friend of him ; and though Adam has fallen, and all his race are depraved, God is still aiming at the same thing, namely, to create holy beings, purified unto himself, to be a peculiar people, zealous for good works. What has the Lord done ? What is he still doing to this end ? How far have we participated in those processes of grace which work towards this glorious design ?

I ask your attention this morning while I speak, first, *of what we were;* and here let the tears stand in your eyes : secondly, *of what has been done for us;* and here let grace move in your hearts : and, thirdly, *of what we wish to do;* and here let care be seen in your lives.

I. First, beloved, let us think for a few minutes only OF WHAT WE ONCE WERE. Think, I say, with tears of repentance in our eyes " For we ourselves also were sometimes foolish, disobedient, deceived, serving divers lusts and pleasures, living in malice and envy, hateful, and hating one another." The apostle does not say, " *Ye* yourselves," as if he spoke to Titus and the believing Cretians, but *we* ourselves, thus including himself. Beloved apostle, thou dost humbly present to us this bitter cup of confession, drinking of it thyself with us, and putting thyself on a level with us—" We ourselves also." Come, then, pastor, elders, deacons, and members of the church, you that have served your Lord for many years, hesitate not to join in this humiliating confession.

A threefold set of evils is here described. The first set consists of *the evils of the mind:* " We were sometimes foolish, disobedient, deceived." We were *foolish.* We thought we knew, and therefore we did not learn. We said, " We see," and therefore we were blind, and would not come to Jesus for sight. We thought we knew better than God ; for our foolish heart was darkened, and we imagined ourselves to be better judges of what was good for us than the Lord our God. We refused heavenly warnings because we dreamed that sin was pleasant and profitable. We rejected divine truth because we did not care to be taught, and disdained the lowly position of a disciple sitting at Jesus' feet. Our pride proved our folly. What lying things we tried to believe! We put bitter for sweet, and sweet for bitter; darkness for light, and light for darkness. In thought, desire, language, and action " we were sometimes foolish." Some of us were manifestly foolish, for we rushed headlong into sins which injured us, and have left that in our bones which years have not been sufficient to remove. Every lover of vice is a fool writ large. O my brother, I suppose you have no photograph of yourself as you used to be; but if you have, take it down, and study it, and bless God that he has made you to differ so greatly from your former self!

In addition to being foolish, we are said to have been *disobedient;* and so we were, for we forsook the commands of God. We wanted our own will and way. We said, " Who is the Lord, that we should obey his voice ? " There is a touch of Pharaoh about every one of us. Obedience is distasteful to the obstinate; and we were such. " I knew," said God, " that thou wast very obstinate, and hadst an iron sinew." Our necks by nature refuse to bow to the yoke of our Creator. We would, if we could, be the lords of providence, for we are not content with the divine allotment. We wish that we were the legislators of the universe, that we might give license to our own lusts, and no longer be hampered with restrictions. To the holy law of God we were disobedient. Ah, how long some of us were disobedient to the gospel! We heard it as though we heard it not; or when it did touch the heart, we did not allow its influence to remain. Like water, which retains no mark of a blow, so did we obliterate the effect of truth. We were determined not to be obedient to the faith of the Lord Jesus. We were unwilling to yield God his due place either in providence, law, or gospel.

Paul adds that we were *deceived,* or led astray. As sheep follow one another, and go away from the pasture, so did we follow some chosen companion, and would not follow the good Shepherd. We were deceived. Perhaps we were deceived in our thoughts, and made to believe a lie; certainly we were deceived in our idea of happiness; we hoped to find it where it does not exist, we searched for the living among the dead. We were the dupes of custom and of company. We were here, there, and everywhere in our actions : no more to be relied upon than lost sheep.

Children of God, remember these errors of your minds, lay them upon your consciences, and let your souls plead guilty to them; for I feel assured that we have all, in some measure, been in this triple condition—foolish, disobedient, deceived.

The next bundle of mischief is found in *the evils of our pursuits.* The apostle says we were " serving divers lusts and pleasures." The word for " serving " means being under servitude. We were once the slaves of divers lusts and pleasures. By *lusts* we understand desires, longings, ambitions, passions. Many are these masters, and they are all tyrants. Some are ruled by greed for money; others crave for fame; some are enslaved by lust for power; others by the lust of the eye; and many by the lusts of the flesh. We were born slaves, and we live slaves until the great Liberator emancipates us. No man can be in worse bondage than to be enslaved by his own evil desires.

We were also the bond-slaves of *pleasure*. Alas! alas! that we were so far infatuated as to call it pleasure! Looking back at our former lives, we may well be amazed that we could once take pleasure in things whereof we are now ashamed. The Lord has taken the very name of our former idols out of our mouths. Some who are now saints were once the slaves of drunkenness, or of "chambering and wantonness." Some were given up to evil company and rioting, or to pride and self-seeking. Many are the evils which array themselves in the silken robes of pleasure, that they may tempt the hungry heart of man. Once we took pleasure in those sins which are now our misery as we look back on them. O my brethren, we dare not deny our base original! To-day we drink from the well of holiness undefiled pleasures which delight our souls; but we blush as we remember that aforetime yonder foul and putrid pools seemed sweet to our vitiated taste. Like Nebuchadnezzar in the failure of his mind, we fed among beasts in the madness of our sin. Unlike the Egyptians, who loathed to drink of the river when God had smitten it with his curse, we took all the more delight in draughts of unhallowed pleasure because it yielded a fearful intoxication to know that we were daring to defy a law.

Do not let me talk about these things this morning while you listen to me without feeling. I want you to be turning over the pages of your old life, and joining with Paul and the rest of us in our sad confession of former pleasure in evil. A holy man was wont to carry with him a book which had three leaves in it, but never a word. The first leaf was black, and this showed his sin; the second was red, and this reminded him of the way of cleansing by blood; while the third was white, to show how clean the Lord can make us. I beg you just now to study that first black page. It is all black; and as you look at it, it shows blacker and blacker. What seemed at one time to be a little white darkens down as it is gazed upon, till it wears the deepest shade of all. Ye were sometimes erring in your minds and in your pursuits. Is not this enough to bring the water into your eyes, O ye that now follow the Lamb whithersoever he goeth?

The apostle then mentions *the evils of our hearts*. Here you must discriminate, and judge, each one for himself, how far the accusation lies. He speaks of "living in malice and envy, hateful and hating one another." That is to say, first, we harboured *anger* against those who had done us evil; and, secondly, we lived in envy of those who appeared to have more good than we had ourselves. The first sin is very common: many abide year after year in the poisonous atmosphere of an angry spirit. All are not alike in this, for some are naturally easy and placable; but in all of us there is that proud spirit which resents injuries, and would revenge them. Men may sin against God, and we are not indignant; but if they sin against us, we are very angry. To the spirit of Christ it is natural and even delightful to forgive: but such is not the spirit of the world. I have heard of men who would not forgive their own children, and of brothers who were implacable towards each other. This is the spirit of the devil. Revenge is the delight of the wicked, but to do kindness in return for injury is the luxury of a Christian. One main distinction between the heirs of God and the heirs of wrath is this : the unregenerate are in the power of self, and so of hate, but the regenerate are under the dominion of Christ, and so of love. Thou mayest judge thyself by this, whether thy prevailing spirit is that of wrath or of love : if thou art given to anger, thou art a child of wrath; and if thou art full of love, thou art a child of God, whose name is *love*. God help us to stamp out the last spark of personal animosity! Let us remove the memories of injury, as the incoming tide washes out the marks on the sand. If any of you have disputes in your family, end them at once, cost what it may. How can you love God whom you have not seen if you do not love your brother whom you have seen ? Grace makes a great change in this respect in those who by nature are malicious.

The other form of evil is. *envy* of those who seem to have more of good than we have. Frequently envy attacks men because of their wealth. How dare they have luxuries when we are poor? At other times envy spits its venom against a man's good repute, when he happens to be more praised than we are. How can any man venture to be better thought of than we are ? Truly this is the spirit of the devil, the spirit which now worketh in the children of disobedience. The child of God is delivered from envy by the grace of God; and if it ever does arise, he hates himself for admitting it. He would wish to see others happy, even if he were unhappy himself. If he be in the depths of poverty, he is glad that everybody is not so pinched as he is. If he has received unjust censure, he is willing to hope that there was some mistake; and he is glad that everybody is not quite so unfairly dealt with. He rejoices in the praise of others, and triumphs in their success. What! do you wince at this, and feel that you have not reached so far? May grace enable you to get into this spirit, for it is the spirit of Jesus!

Beloved, sin takes different shapes in different people, but it is in us all. This darkness once beclouded those who to-day shine like stars among the godly. Sin is often restrained by circumstances, and yet it is in the heart. We ought not to take credit to ourselves because of our freedom from evils into which we had no chance of falling. We have not been so bad as others because we could not be. A certain boy has run away from home. Another boy remained at home. Is he, therefore, a better child? Listen! he had broken his leg, and could not get out of bed. That takes away all the credit of his staying at home. Some men cannot sin in a certain direction, and then they say to themselves, "What excellent fellows we are to abstain from this wickedness!" Sirs, you would have done it if you could, and therefore your self-praise is mere flattery. Had you been placed in the same position as others, you would have acted as others have done, for your heart goes after the same idols. Sin in the heart of every man defiles everything that he does. Even if an ungodly man should do what in itself might be a good action, there is a defilement in his motive which taints it all. You cannot draw pure water from a foul well. As is the heart, such is the life. Listen to this, ye that have never passed under the processes of divine grace. See what you are, and where you are, if left to yourselves, and cry to the Lord to save you.

II. Now for a more cheerful topic. We are now to think OF WHAT HAS BEEN DONE FOR US; and here let us feel the movements of grace in our hearts. What has been done for us?

First, *there was a divine interposition.* "The kindness and love of God our Saviour toward man appeared." Man was in the dark, plunging onward to blacker midnight every step he took. I do not find, as I read history, any excuse for the modern notion that men are longing for God, and labouring to find him. No, the sheep were never seeking the Shepherd, but all were going astray. Men everywhere turn their backs to the light, and try to forget what has been handed down by their forefathers: they are everywhere feeling after a great lie which they may raise to the throne of God. We do not by nature long after God, nor sigh for his holiness. The gracious Lord came in uncalled for and unsought, and in the bounty of his heart, and in the great love of his nature, he determined to save man. Methinks I hear him say, "How shall I give thee up?" He sees mankind resolved to perish unless an almighty arm shall intervene; and he interposes in fulness of pity and power. You know how, in many ways, the Lord has intervened on our behalf; but, especially, you remember how he came down from heaven, took our nature, lived among us, mourned our sin, and bore it in his own body on the tree. You know how the Son of God interposed in that grand *Avatar*, that marvellous incarnation in which the Word became flesh, and dwelt among us. Then broke he what would else have been an everlasting darkness; then snapped he the chain which must have fettered our humanity throughout all the ages. The love and kindness of God our Saviour, which had always existed, at length "appeared" when God, in the person of his Son, came hither, met our iniquities hand to hand, and overcame their terrible power, that we also might overcome.

Note well that *there was a divine salvation.* In consequence of the interposition of Jesus, believers are described as being saved: "not by works of righteousness which we have done, but according to his mercy he saved us." Hearken to this. There are men in the world who are saved: they are spoken of, not as "to be saved," not as to be saved when they come to die, but saved even now—saved from the dominion of the evils which we described under our first head: saved from folly, disobedience, delusion, and the like. Whosoever believeth in the Lord Jesus Christ, whom God has set forth to be the propitiation for sin, is saved from the guilt and power of sin. He shall no longer be the slave of his lusts and pleasures; he is saved from that dread bondage. He is saved from hate, for he has tasted love, and learned to love. He shall not be condemned for all that he has hitherto done, for his great Substitute and Saviour has borne away the guilt, the curse, the punishment of sin; yea, and sin itself. O my hearer, if thou believest in the Lord Jesus Christ this morning, thou art saved! As surely as once thou wast lost, being led astray, so surely art thou now saved, if thou art a believer, being found by the great Shepherd, and brought back again upon his shoulders. I beg you to get hold of this truth, that according to his mercy the Lord has saved us who believe in Jesus. Will you tell me, or rather tell yourselves, whether you are saved or not? If you are not saved, you are lost; if you are not already forgiven, you are already condemned. You are in the ruin of fallen nature, unless you are renewed by the Holy Ghost. You are a slave to sin, unless your liberty has been procured by the great ransom. Examine yourselves on these points, and follow me in the next thought.

There was a motive for this salvation. Positively, " According to his mercy he saved us "; and negatively, " Not by works of righteousness which we have done." Brethren, we could not have been saved at the first by our works of righteousness; for we had not done any. " No," says the apostle, " we were foolish, disobedient, deceived," and therefore we had no works of righteousness, and yet the Lord interposed and saved us. Behold and admire the splendour of his love, that " He loved us even when we were dead in sins." He loved us, and therefore quickened us. God does not come to men to help them when they are saving themselves; but he comes to the rescue when they are damning themselves. When the heart is full of folly and disobedience, the good God visits it with his favour. He comes, not according to the hopefulness of our character, but according to his mercy; and mercy has no eye except for guilt and misery. The grace of God is not even given according to any good thing that we have done since our conversion: the expression before us shuts out all real works of righteousness which we have done since regeneration, as all supposed ones before it. The Lord assuredly foreknew these works, but he also foreknew our sins. He did not save us according to the foreknowledge of our good works, because these works are a part of the salvation which he gave us. As well say that a physician healed a sick man, because he foreknew that he would be better; or that you give a beggar an alms, because you foresee that he would have the alms. Works of righteousness are the fruit of salvation, and the root must come before the fruit. The Lord saves his people out of clear, unmixed, undiluted mercy and grace, and for no other reason. " I will have mercy on whom I will have mercy, and I will have compassion on whom I will have compassion. So then it is not of him that willeth, nor of him that runneth, but of God that sheweth mercy." Oh, how splendidly is the grace of God seen in the whole plan of salvation! How clearly is it seen in our cases, for " we ourselves also were sometimes foolish, disobedient, deceived," yet he saved us, " not by works of righteousness which we have done, but according to his mercy"! Will not some self-convicted sinner find comfort here? O despairing one, does not a little hope come in by this window? Do you not see that God can save you on the ground of mercy? He can wash you and renew you according to the sovereignty of his grace. On the footing of merit you are hopelessly lost, but on the ground of mercy there is hope.

Observe, next, that *there was a power by which we were saved.* " He saved us by the washing of regeneration, and renewing of the Holy Ghost; which he shed on us abundantly through Jesus Christ our Saviour." The way in which we are delivered from the dominion of sin is by the work of the Holy Ghost. This adorable Person is very

God of very God. This divine Being comes to us, and causes us to be born again. By his eternal power and Godhead, he gives us a totally new nature, a life which could not grow out of our former life, nor be developed from our nature—a life which is a new creation of God. We are saved, not by evolution, but by creation. The Spirit of God creates us anew in Christ Jesus unto good works. We experience regeneration, which means—being generated over again, or born again. Remember the result of this as set forth in covenant terms—"A new heart also will I give you, and a new spirit will I put within you: and I will take away the stony heart out of your flesh, and I will give you an heart of flesh." This great process is carried out by the Holy Ghost.

After we are regenerated, he continues to renew us; our thoughts, feelings, desires, and acts are constantly renewed. Regeneration as the commencement of the new creation can never come twice to any man, but renewal of the Holy Ghost is constantly and perpetually repeated. The life once given is revived: the light once kindled is fed with holy oil, which is poured upon it continually. The new-born life is deepened and increased in force by that same Holy Spirit who first of all created it. See then, dear hearers, that the only way to holiness is to be made anew, and to be kept anew. The washing of regeneration and the renewing of the Holy Ghost are both essential. The name of Jesus has been engraved in us, even on our hearts, but it needs to be cut deeper and deeper, lest the letters be covered up by the moss of routine, or filled up by the bespatterings of sin. We are saved "by the washing of regeneration and renewing of the Holy Ghost"—one process in different stages. This is what our God has done for us: blessed be his name! Being washed and renewed we are saved.

There is also mentioned a blessed privilege which comes to us by Jesus Christ. The Spirit is shed on us abundantly by Jesus Christ, and we are "justified by his grace." Both justification and sanctification come to us through the medium of our Lord Jesus Christ. The Holy Spirit is shed on us abundantly "through Jesus Christ our Saviour." Beloved, never forget that regeneration is wrought in us by the Holy Spirit, but comes to us by Jesus Christ. We do not receive any blessing apart from our Lord Jesus. In all works of the Spirit, whether regeneration or renewal, it is the Lord Jesus who is putting forth his power, for he saith, "Behold, I make all things new." The Mediator is the conduit-pipe through which grace supplies us day by day with the water of life. Everything is by Jesus Christ. Without him was not anything made that was made, either in grace or in nature. We must not think it possible for us to receive anything from God apart from the appointed Mediator. But, oh, think of it! —in Jesus Christ we are to-day abundantly anointed by the Holy Spirit; the sacred oil is shed upon us abundantly from him who is our Head. We are sweet to God through the divine perfume of the Holy Spirit who comes to us by Jesus Christ. This day we are just in the sight of God in Christ's righteousness, through which we are "justified by grace." Jehovah sees no sin for which he must punish us; he has said, "Take away his filthy garments from him, and set a fair mitre upon his head"; and this is done. We are accepted in the Beloved.

Since Jesus has washed our feet, we are "clean every whit"—clean in the double sense of being washed with water and with blood, and so cleansed from the power and guilt of sin. What a high privilege is this! Can we ever sufficiently praise God for it?

Once more, *there comes out of this a divine result.* We become to-day joint-heirs with Christ Jesus, and so heirs of a heavenly estate; and then out of this heirship there grows a hope which reaches forward to the eternal future with exceeding joy. We are "made heirs according to the hope of eternal life." Think of that! What a space there is between "foolish, disobedient, deceived"—right up to "heirs according to the hope of eternal life"! Who thought of bridging this great gulf? Who but God? With what power did he bridge it? How, but by the divine power and Godhead of the Holy Ghost? Where was the bridge found by which the chasm could be crossed? The cross of our Lord Jesus Christ, who loved us and gave himself for us, has made a way over the once impassable deep.

I have thus very briefly set before you an outline of the work of grace within the human heart. Do you understand it? Have you ever felt it? Do you feel the life of regeneration pulsing within you this morning? Will you not bless God for it?

> " We raise our Father's name on high,
> Who his own Spirit sends
> To bring rebellious strangers nigh,
> And turn his foes to friends."

III. We will now speak OF WHAT WE WISH TO DO; and here let us show care in our lives. Mark well these words, "This is a faithful saying, and these things I will that thou affirm constantly, that they which have believed in God might be careful to maintain good works. These things are good and profitable unto men."

"Be careful to maintain good works." This precept is *full in its meaning.* In another Scripture you are told to be careful for nothing, but here you are bidden to be careful to maintain good works. We read, "casting all your care upon him; for he careth for you": but do not cast off your care to maintain good works. You have a number of cares about you; slip a bridle over their heads, and train them to plough in the field of good works. Do not let care be wasted over food and raiment and such temporary matters—these may be left with God; but take sacred cares upon you—the cares of holy and gracious living. Yoke your best thoughts to the car of holiness—"be careful to maintain good works."

What are good works? The term is greatly inclusive. Of course we number in the list works of charity, works of kindness and benevolence, works of piety, reverence, and holiness. Such works as comply with the two tables of command are good works. Works of obedience are good works. What you do because God bids you do it, is a good work. Works of love to Jesus, done out of a desire for his glory, these are good works. The common actions of every-day life, when they are well done, with a view not to merit, but out of gratitude—these are good works. "Be careful to maintain good works" of every sort and kind. You are sure to be working in some way, mind that your works are good works. If you have commenced well, be careful to *maintain* good works; and if you have maintained them, go on to increase them. I preached last Thursday night as now —salvation by grace, and by grace alone; and if I know how to speak plainly, I certainly did speak plainly then, and I hope I do so now. Remember, you are saved by grace, and not by works of righteousness; but after you are saved there comes in this precept, "Be careful to maintain good works."

This precept is *special in its direction*. To the sinner, that he may be saved, we say not a word concerning good works, except to remind him that he has none of them. To the believer who is saved, we say ten thousand words concerning good works, beseeching him to bring forth much fruit, that so he may be Christ's disciple. There is all the difference between the living and the dead: the living we arouse to work; the dead must first receive life. Exhortations which may most fittingly be addressed to the regenerate may be quite out of place when spoken to those who are under the power of unbelief, and are strangers to the family of grace. The voice of our text is to them that have believed in God; faith is pre-supposed as the absolutely indispensable foundation of good works. You cannot work that which will please God if you are without faith in him. As there is no coming to God in prayer without believing that he is and that he is the rewarder of them that diligently seek him, so there is no bringing any other sacrifice to him without a faith suitable to the business in hand. For living works you must have a living faith, and for loving works you must have a loving faith. When we know and trust God, then with holy intelligence and sacred confidence we work his pleasure. Good works must be done freely: God wants not slaves to grace his throne; he seeks not from us the forced works of men in bondage. He desires the spontaneous zeal of consecrated souls who rejoice to do his will, because they are not their own, but bought with the precious blood of Jesus. It is the heartiness of our work which is the heart of it. To those who have renewed hearts, this exhortation is addressed—"Be careful to maintain good works."

This precept is *weighty in importance*, for it is prefaced thus: "This is a faithful saying." This is one among four great matters thus described. It is not trivial, it is not a temporary precept which belongs to an extinct race and a past age. "This is a faithful saying"—a true Christian proverb, "that they which have believed in God might be careful to maintain good works." Let the ungodly never say that we who believe in free grace think lightly of a holy life. O you who are the people of my care, I charge you before God and the holy angels that, in proportion as you hold the truth of doctrine, you follow out the purity of precept! You hold the truth, and you know that salvation is not of man, nor of man's work: it is not of merit, but of mercy, not of ourselves, but of God alone; I beseech you to be as right in practice as in doctrine, and therefore be careful to maintain good works. Dogs will open their mouths, but do not find bones for them: the enemies of the faith will cavil at it, but do not give them ground of accusation. May God the Holy Spirit help you so to live that they may be ashamed, having no evil thing to say of you!

I am afraid that this precept of being careful to maintain good works is *neglected in practice,* or else the apostle would not have said to Titus, " These things I will that thou affirm constantly." Titus must repeat perpetually the precept which commands the careful maintenance of good works. Beloved, I fear that preachers often think too well of their congregations, and talk to them as if they were all perfect, or nearly so. I cannot thus flatter you. I have been astounded when I have seen what professing Christians can do. How some dare call themselves followers of Jesus I cannot tell! It is horrible. We condemn Judas, but his fellow is to be found in many. Our Lord is still sold for gain. He still has at his heels sons of perdition who kiss him and betray him. There are still persons in our churches who need to have the ten commandments read to them every Sabbath-day. It is not a bad plan of the Church of England, to put up the ten commandments near the communion table where they can be clearly seen. Some people need to see them; though I am afraid, when they come in their way, they wink hard at some of the commands, and go away and forget that they have seen them. Common morality is neglected by some who call themselves Christians.

My brethren, such things ought not to be, but as long as they are so we must hear Paul saying: " I will that thou affirm constantly that they which have believed in God might be careful to maintain good works." Certain people turn on their heel, and say, " That is legal talk. The preacher is preaching up works instead of grace." What! will you dare to say that? I will meet you face to face at God's right hand at the last day if you dare to insinuate so gross a libel. Dare you say that I do not preach continually salvation by the grace of God, and by the grace of God only? Having preached salvation by grace without a moment's hesitation, I shall also continually affirm that they which have believed in God must be " careful to maintain good works."

This, mark you, is *supported by argument.* The apostle presses home his precept by saying: " These things are good and profitable unto men." He instances other things which are neither good nor profitable, namely, " Foolish questions, and genealogies, and contentions, and strivings about the law." In these days some are occupied with questions about the future state, instead of accepting the plain testimony of Scripture, and some give more prominence to speculations drawn from prophecy than to the maintaining of good works. I reverence the prophecies ; but I have small patience with those whose one business is guessing at their meaning. One whose family was utterly unruly and immoral met with a Christian friend, and said to him : " Do you quite see the meaning of the Seven Trumpets? " " No," answered his friend, " I do not; and if you looked more to your seven children the seven trumpets would suffer no harm." To train up your children and instruct your servants, and order your household aright, are " things which are good and profitable unto men." A life of godliness is better than the understanding of mysteries. The eternal truth of God is to be defended at all hazards, but questions which do not signify the turn of a hair to either God or man may be left to settle themselves. " Be careful to maintain good works," whether you are a babe in grace or a strong man in Christ Jesus. A holy household is as a pillar to the church of God. Children brought up in the fear of God are as cornerstones polished after the similitude of a palace. You, husbands and wives, that live together in holy love, and see your children serving God, you adorn the doctrine of God our Saviour! Tradesmen who are esteemed for integrity, merchants who bargain to their own hurt but change not, dealers who can be trusted in the market with uncounted gold, your acts are good and profitable both to the church and to the world! Men are won to Christ when they see Christianity embodied in the good and the true. But when religion is a thin veneer or a mere touch of tinsel, they call it "humbug"; and rough as the word is, it is worthy of the contemptible thing which it describes. If our religion comes from the very soul, if our life is the life of Christ in us, and we prove that we have new hearts and right spirits by acting the honourable, the kindly, the truly Christian part, these things are good and profitable unto those who watch us, for they may induce them to seek for better things.

I pray you, my beloved, be careful to maintain good works. I thus stir up your pure minds by way of remembrance: if your minds were not pure I would not stir them up, for it would be of no use to raise the mud which now lies quiet. I stir you up because I am not afraid to do so, but am sure that it will do you good. You will take home this exhortation, and you will say, each one to himself, "What can I do more for Jesus? How can I walk more worthy of my profession? How can I be careful to maintain good works?" So may God bless you!

You who do not believe in God, who have not come to trust in his dear Son, I am not talking to you. To you, I must say, first, that you must be made new creatures. I do not talk to a crab-tree, and say, "Bear apples." It cannot. The tree must first become good before the fruit can be good. "Ye must be born again." You will never be better till you are made new creatures. You must be spiritually slain, and then made alive again. There must be an end of you, and there must be a beginning of Christ in you. God grant that this may happen at once, and may you immediately believe in the Lord Jesus! Amen.

Life and Pardon

"And you, being dead in your sins and the uncircumcision of your flesh, hath he quickened together with him, having forgiven you all trespasses."—Colossians ii. 13.

THE teaching of this verse is much the same as that in preceding verses; but the apostle does not hesitate to dwell again and again upon the important matters of quickening and forgiveness. These lie in the foundation. Ministers of Christ cannot too often go over the essential points : their hearers cannot too often hear vital truths. Our frail memories and dull understandings require line upon line, precept upon precept, in reference to fundamental truths : our apprehension of them is far too feeble, and can never be too vivid.

To find instances of the work of God in quickening souls and in pardoning sins, Paul does not look far afield. In the text he says, "*And you,*" and, according to the Revised Version, he repeats the word further on, and the passage runs thus, "You, being dead through your trespasses and the uncircumcision of your flesh, *you, I say*, did he quicken together with him." He points personally to the saints at Colosse. We are not about to consider a prophecy to be fulfilled in the millennium, neither are we speaking of matters which concern the unknown dwellers in the moon. No; the theme belongs to you, to you, I say, if indeed you be the people of God. You are speci-mens of the divine work: *you* hath he quickened, *you* hath he par-doned. It is profitable for us to be engaged upon matters which concern us. I shall speak to you of those things which I have tasted and handled of the good word of life, and it is my firm belief that, to the most of you, these matters are familiar in your mouths as household words. If not, I grieve over you. Let none of us be content unless the works of the Holy Spirit are manifest in us. What boots it to me if another man receive life and pardon, if I am cast for death, and lie still under condemnation ? Press forward, my beloved, to a personal enjoyment of these chief blessings of the covenant of grace— life in Jesus, forgiveness through his blood. Let every part of the sermon have a finger pointed at yourselves. Hear it speak to you, even to you.

In the text we have the conjunction of two things—quickening and forgiveness. We will consider these things in connection with each other. Their order it may be difficult to lay down: in the text they are described as if they were the same thing. Which comes first, the impartation of the new life, or the blotting out of sin? Is not pardon first? Doth God pardon a dead man? How can he give the life which is the proof of pardon to the man who is not forgiven? On the other hand, if a man has not spiritual life sufficient to make him feel his guilt, how can he cry for pardon? And if it be unsought, how shall it be received? A man may be spiritually alive so as to be groaning under the pollution and the burden of sin, and yet he may not have received by faith the remission of sins. In the order of our experience, the reception of life comes before the enjoyment of pardon. We are made to live spiritually, and so we are made to repent, to confess, to believe, and to receive forgiveness. First, the life which sighs under sin, and then the life which sings concerning pardon. Misery is first felt, and then mercy is received.

Following the line of experience, we shall notice concerning the favoured ones of God, first, *what they were:* "You, being dead in your sins and the uncircumcision of your flesh." Secondly, we shall note *what has been done in them:* "Hath he quickened together with him"; and then, thirdly, *what he hath done for them:* "Having forgiven you all trespasses." May the Holy Ghost lead us into these truths, and give us the life of God and the rest of faith!

I. First, then, consider WHAT THEY WERE. Beloved, they were all by nature children of wrath, even as others. There is no distinction in the condition of natural men before the law. We all fell in Adam. We are all gone out of the way, and have all become unprofitable. Any difference which now exists has been made by divine grace; but by nature we are all in the same condemnation, and all tainted by the same depravity.

Where were we when the Lord first looked on us? Answer.—We were *dead according to the sentence of the law.* The Lord had said, "In the day that thou eatest thereof thou shalt surely die"; and Adam did die the moment that he ate of the forbidden fruit, and his posterity died in him. What is death natural? It is the separation of the body from the soul, which is its life. What is death spiritual? It is the separation of the soul from God, who is its life. It had been the very life of Adam to be united to God; and when he lost his union of heart with God, his spirit underwent a dreadful death. This death is upon each one of us by nature. Above this comes in the dreadful fact, that "He that believeth not is condemned already." The position of every unbeliever is that of one who is dead by law. As far as the liberties, and privileges, and enjoyments of heavenly things are concerned, he is written among the dead. His name is registered among the condemned. Yet, beloved, while we are under the sentence of death, the Lord comes to us in almighty grace, and quickens us into newness of life, forgiving us all trespasses. Are you trembling because of your condemned condition under the law? Do you recognize the tremendous truth that death is the sure and righteous result of sin? Then to you, even to you, the life-giving, pardoning word is sent in the preaching of the everlasting gospel. Oh that you may believe, and so escape from condemnation!

These favoured people were *dead through the action of their sin.* Sin stupefies and kills. Where it reigns, the man is utterly insensible to spiritual truth, feeling, and action; he is dead to everything that is holy in the sight of God. He may have keen moral perceptions, but he has no spiritual feelings. Men differ widely as to their moral qualities; all men are not alike bad, especially when measured in reference to their fellow-men; some may even be excellent and praise-worthy, viewed from that standpoint. But to *spiritual* things all men are alike dead. Look at the multitude of our hearers; to what purpose do we preach to them? You may declare the wrath of God against the godless, but what do they care? You may speak of Jesus' love to the lost; how little it affects them! Sin is not horrible, and salvation is not precious, to them. They may not controvert your teaching; but they have no sensible apprehension of truth: it does not come home to them as a matter of any consequence. Let eternal things drift as they may, they are perfectly content so long as they can answer those three questions—"What shall we eat? what shall we drink? and wherewithal shall we be clothed?" No higher question troubles their earth-bound minds. They may entertain some liking towards theological study and Bible-teaching, as a matter of education; but they do not view the truths revealed in Scripture as matters of overwhelming importance. They trifle; they delay; they set on one side the things which make for their peace. Their religion has no influence upon their thoughts and actions: they are dead. Sin has slain them. I see them mingled with this great congregation like corpses sitting upright among the living. I look out upon the masses of this vast city and upon the innumerable hosts of populous countries, and I see a measureless cemetery, a dread domain of death; a region without life.

One point must be noticed here, which makes this spiritual death the more terrible: *they are dead, but yet responsible.* If men were literally dead, then they were incapable of sin; but the kind of death of which we speak involves a responsibility none the less, but all the greater. If I say of a man that he is such a liar that he cannot speak the truth, do you therefore think him blameless? No; but you judge him to be all the more worthy of condemnation because he has lost the very sense which discerns between a truth and a lie. If we say of a certain man, as we have had to do, "He is a rogue ingrained; he is so tricky that he cannot deal honestly, but must always be cheating"; do you therefore excuse his fraud, and pity him? Far from it. His inability is not physical, but moral inability, and is the con-sequence of his own persistence in evil. The law is as much binding upon the morally incapable as upon the most sanctified in nature. If, through a man's own perversity, he wills to reject good and love evil, the blame is with himself. He is said to be dead in sin, not in the sense that he is irresponsible, but in the sense that he is so evil that he will not keep the law of God. If a man were brought to-morrow before the Lord Mayor, and he were accused of theft; suppose he should say, "My lord, I ought to be set free, for I am such a rascal that I cannot see an article in a shop but what my fingers itch to lay hold upon it "; would not the judge give such a worthless person all the more punishment? O sinners, dead in sin, you are not so dead as thereby to be free from the guilt of breaking God's command, and rejecting Christ; but you heap upon yourselves mountains of guilt every day that you abide in this condition.

The ungodly are so dead as to be careless as to their state. Indeed, all gracious things are despised of them. Sometimes they attend religious services; but they get angry if the preacher presses them too hard. I have known them vow that they will never hear the man again because he is so personal. Pray, sirs, what is a preacher to be but personal? If he shoots, is he to have no target, and take no aim? What is our very office and business for, but to deal personally with you about your sins? In ungodly men there is an utter reckless-ness as to their condition before God. They know that they may die, they know that if they die they will be lost; but they try to forget these facts. The ostrich is said to bury its head in the sand so as not to see the hunter, and then to fancy that it is safe. Thus do men fancy that, by forgetting the danger, they escape it. Some of you have lived in carelessness until grey hairs are on your head. Will you still risk your souls? Alas, you look more anxiously after a battered sixpence, which you miss from your pocket, than after your immortal soul! If you miss a ring from your finger while sitting here, you are more concerned about it than about your eternal destiny. How foolish! How dead are you to all just judgment and prudence! It is your soul, your own soul, your only soul, your never-dying soul, to which we beg you to pay attention, and yet you can hardly have patience with us. If a prisoner in the condemned cell had no sort of care whether he should be set free or hanged, but could even joke about the scaffold and the executioner, you would feel that only by an extreme act of mercy could such a person be pardoned. Nay, if he cares nothing for the penalty, let him bear it: so man would say, and there would be justice in it. Yet God spake not so in reference to some of us; for while we were in a condition of callous-ness the grace of God came to us, and by quickening us, gave us to be anxious, and led us to pray.

The text adds that we were *dead in the uncircumcision of our flesh.* I need not dwell upon the external figure here employed; its meaning is clear enough. The uncircumcision of our flesh means that we were not in covenant with God: it shows also the abiding of our filthiness upon us; the willingness of our souls to be aliens from the common-wealth of Israel, without God in the world. This is where we were in the uncircumcision of our flesh; and yet the grace of God found us out. Oh, I could paint the man! He is anxious about this world, but what cares he for the world to come? He is a master of his own trade, and he prospers in it; but for his God, and his service, he spares not an hour's consideration. He cries, "The covenant of grace, what is that?" And he turns on his heel, like Pilate, when he had said, "What is truth?" As to having any sense of the constant presence of God, and his deep indebtedness to God, and of the sweetness of being pardoned, and the bliss of enjoying the love of God, and walking with

God, he has no notion, or, at best, he cries, "Oh, yes, that is all very fine for those who have nothing else to do; let them find delight in it if they can!" To him God is nothing, heaven is nothing, hell less than nothing. He passes by Calvary itself, where God in human flesh is bleeding out redemption, and it is nothing to him. The wail from the cross he never hears, though it asks him this question—"Is it nothing to you, all ye that pass by? behold, and see if there be any sorrow like unto my sorrow!" What cares he for the wounds of his soul's best lover? He has no concern about any purchase made by the Redeemer, or of any death especially on his behalf, or any resurrection with Christ which he may hope to enjoy. The man is dead to faith, and glory, and immortality. The low and the grovelling charm him, but the pure and the noble find him dead to their claims. Yet to such, even to such, does sovereign grace approach. Unbought, unsought, it cometh according to that word of Scripture, "I am found of them that sought me not."

Again, spiritually the ungodly are *dead, and utterly incapable of obtaining life for themselves.* Could any of you, with the utmost diligence, create life, even the lowest form of it? To a man who is dead, could you impart life? You might galvanize his limbs into a kind of motion; but real life, the pulsing of the heart, the heaving of the lungs, could you create it? You know you cannot! Much less can the dead man himself create life within himself. The man without Christ is utterly unable to quicken himself. We are "without strength," unable to do anything as of ourselves, and while we are in this condition grace comes to us.

Alas, there remains one more point! Man may be described as *dead and becoming corrupt.* After a while the dead body shows symptoms of decay: this is vice in its beginning. Leave the corpse where it is, and it will become putrid, polluting the air, and disgusting every sense of the living. "Bury my dead out of my sight," is the cry of the most affectionate mother or wife. And so it is with many ungodly men. Some of them are restrained from the grosser vices, just as Egyptian bodies were, by spices, preserved from rottenness. By example, by instruction, by fear, by surroundings, many are kept from the more putrid sins, and therefore are not so obnoxious to society. Towards God they are dead as ever; but towards man they are no more objectionable than the mummies in yonder cases in the British Museum. But this embalming of the dead with spices of morality, has not been carried out with hosts of those around us. They rot above ground: their blasphemies pollute the air, their lewdness infects our streets, their revelry makes night hideous. The tendency of dead flesh is towards the corruption which shows itself in loathesome actions. The mercy is, that where even this has taken place, where the foul worm of vice has begun its awful work, in drunkenness, in blasphemy, in dishonesty, or in uncleanness of life—even there the quickening Spirit can come. As life came to Lazarus, who had been dead four days, so can spiritual life come to those who have fallen into the noisomeness of open transgression. Leaving this painful matter, let us be filled with deep humility; for such were we in days not long since: but let us also be filled with hope for others; for he who quickened us can do the same for them.

II. And now, secondly, WHAT HAS BEEN DONE IN US? What hath God wrought?

We have been quickened. To tell you, exactly, how quickening is worked in us, is quite beyond my power. The Holy Spirit comes to a man when he is dead in sin, and he breathes into him a new and mysterious life. We do not know how we receive our natural life: how the soul comes into the body we know not. Do you suppose that spiritual life in its beginning will be less mysterious? Did not our Lord say, "The wind bloweth where it listeth, and thou hearest the sound thereof, but canst not tell whence it cometh, and whither it goeth: so is every one that is born of the Spirit"? Thou knowest not the way of the Spirit, nor how he breathes eternal life. We know, however, that as soon as life comes, our first feeling is one of pain and uneasiness. In the case of persons who have been nearly drowned, when they begin to revive they experience very unpleasant sensations. Certainly the parallel holds good in spiritual things. Now, the man sees sin to be an exceeding great evil. He is startled by the discovery of its foulness. He was told all about it, and yet he knew nothing to purpose; but now sin becomes a load, a pain, a horror. As dead, he felt no weight; but as quickened, he groans beneath a load. Now he begins to cry, "O wretched man that I am! who shall deliver me?" Now the angels see him on his knees in private. Behold, he prayeth! "God be merciful to me a sinner," is his hourly sigh. Now, also, he begins to struggle against his evil habits: he addicts himself to Bible reading, to praying, and to hearing the Word of God. He is for a while desperately earnest. Alas, he goes back to his old sin! Yet he cannot rest: again he seeks the Lord. With some men a large part of their early spiritual life has been taken up with agonizing strivings and painful endeavours to free themselves from the chains of sin. They have had to learn their weakness by their failures; but the grace of God has not failed. Some, even for years after their conviction by the Spirit of God, have had no comfortable sense of pardon, but very much conflict with sin: yet, still, the life of God has never been utterly quenched within them. Their struggles have proved that the heavenly germ was alive, and was painfully resisting the forces of evil. Men themselves act as if they tried to put out the light which grace has kindled; but they cannot effect their purpose. When once they have been disturbed in their nest, the Lord has not allowed them to settle down in it again. Their once sweet sin has become bitter as wormwood to them. We have known men under conviction go further into sin to drown their convictions; just as a whale, when harpooned, will dive into the depths. But they come up again, and again are wounded: they cannot escape. In the biography of a man of God, who in his early days was a terrible drunkard, we find that, in struggling against intoxication, he was frequently beaten; and there appears in his diary a long blank of which he says, "Four years and a half elapsed, and no account rendered! What can have been the cause of this chasm? Sin! Yes, sin of the blackest dye, of the deepest ingratitude to the Father of mercies!" The wanderer was restless and unhappy in sin. The life within was, like Jonah, thrown into the depths of the sea; but it hated its condition, and struggled to rise out of it. God will not leave the life he has given, even under the worst conditions.

But quickening leads to far more than this. By-and-by the new life exercises its holy senses, and is more clearly seen to be life. The man begins to see that his only hope is in Christ, and he tries humbly to hide himself beneath the merit of the Lord Jesus. He does not dare to say, "I am saved," but he deeply feels that if ever he is saved it must be through the blood and righteousness of the Lord Jesus. Now also he begins to pray, pleading the precious blood; now he hopes, and his hope looks only through the windows of his Lord's wounds. He looks for mercy only through the atoning sacrifice. By-and-by he comes to trust that this mercy has really come to him, and that Jesus had him on his heart when he suffered on the tree. By a desperate effort he throws himself on Christ, and determines to lie at his feet, and, if he must perish, to perish looking unto Jesus. This is a glorious resolve. See him after a while as he rises up into peace, and joy, and consecration! His life now being joined to that of his Lord, he rejoices that he is never to be separated from him. I think I hear him say, "I see it all now. The Lord Jesus bore my sin and carried it away. I died because he died. I live because he lives. The Lord accepts me, because he accepts his Son, and thus I am ' accepted in the Beloved.' "

Henceforth the quickened man tries to live for Christ, out of gratitude; this is the nature of the life he has received. He strives to grow up into Christ, and to become like his Lord in all things. Henceforth he and his Lord are linked together in an everlasting union, and the cause of Jesus is the one thing for which he lives, and for which he would be content to die. Blessed be God, I am not talking any new things to you : you know what I mean. For these forty years have I felt these things, and many of you have felt them longer still. At first the struggling light within you revealed to you nothing but your darkness ; but now you see Jesus, and see yourselves alive in him with a life eternal and heavenly. Blessed be the Lord who hath raised Jesus from the dead, and hath quickened us in him and with him!

III. Now we come to the third point, upon which I pray for a renewed unction from the Holy One. Let us consider, in the last place, WHAT HAS BEEN DONE FOR US : "Having forgiven you all trespasses." Believing in Christ Jesus, I am absolved. I am clear, I am clear before the Lord. "There is therefore now no condemnation to them which are in Christ Jesus." This is the most joyful theme that I can bring before you. And I want you to notice, first, that *pardon is a divine act.* "Having forgiven all trespasses." Who does that ? Why, he that quickened you. I showed just now that none could quicken a dead man but God only ; for the giving of life is an act which is exclusively the Lord's own : and the same God who gives us spiritual life also grants us pardon from his throne. He sovereignly dispenses pardons. We need not go to any human priest to seek absolution, for we may go at once to God who alone hath sovereign right to execute the death-sentence or to pardon the offender. He alone can grant it with sure effect. If any man should say, *absolvo te* (I absolve thee), I would take it for what it was worth, and its worth would not be much. But if HE saith it, who is the Law-giver, and the supreme King; if HE saith it, against whom I have offended, then am I happy indeed. Glory be to his name, who is a God ready to pardon! What bliss I have received in receiving forgiveness from God! Oh, my hearer, if you have done wrong to your fellow-man, ask his forgiveness, as you are bound to do; and if you get it, be thankful, and feel as if a weight were removed from your conscience. But, after all, what is this compared with being forgiven all trespasses by God himself? This can calm the ruffled sea of the soul; yea, still its fiercest tempest. This can make you sleep at nights, instead of tossing to and fro upon a pillow, which conscience turns to stone beneath your aching head. This gives the gleaming eye, the beaming face, the bounding heart. This brings heaven down to earth, and lifts us near to heaven. The Lord hath blotted out our sins, and thus he has removed the bitterest fountain of our sorrows. Pardon from God is a charter of liberty, a testament of felicity.

God's pardon is a gift most free. Look at the text, and note that this pardon comes to persons who are dead in sin. They were utterly unworthy, and did not even seek mercy. The Lord who comes to men when they are dead in sin, comes to quicken them and to pardon them; not because they are ready, but because HE is ready. Hearken, O man! If in thy bosom there is at this moment a great stone instead of a heart of flesh; if thou art paralyzed as to all good things; if there is only enough life in thee to make thee feel thy terrible incapacity for holiness and fellowship with God, yet God can pardon thee, even as thou art, and where thou art. We were in that condition, my brethren, when the Lord came to us in love. "When we were yet without strength, in due time Christ died for the ungodly." We saw that Jesus died, we believed in him as able to save, and we received the forgiveness of sins. Forgiveness is free. The Lord looks for no good thing in the sinner; but he gives him every good thing. O my hearer, if the Lord looked for good in thee, he could not find it. He looks for nothing thou canst do, and nothing thou canst feel, and nothing thou canst resolve to do or feel; but he shows mercy because he delighteth in mercy. He passes by iniquity, transgression, and sin, because it is his nature to be gracious. The cause of divine pardon is in God himself, and in his dear Son. It is not in thee, O sinner! Being dead in the uncircumcision of thy flesh, what canst thou do? He quickens thee and he pardons thee; yea, he is all in all to thee. Wonders of grace! When I get upon this subject I do not need to give you illustrations, nor to find out choice phrases; the glorious fact stands forth in its own native beauty: infinite pardon from an infinite God, given because of his own mercifulness and the merit of his beloved Son, and not because of anything whatsoever in the man whom he pardons. "But the man repents," says one. Yes, I know; but God gives him repentance. "But he confesses sin." Yes, I know it; for the Lord leads him to acknowledge his trespasses. All and everything which looks like a condition of pardon, is also given by the free and sovereign grace of God, and given freely, without money and without price.

I want you to notice *how universal is this pardon* in reference to all sin: "Having forgiven you *all* trespasses." Consult your memory, and think of all your trespasses, if you dare. That one black night! Has it left a crimson spot, indelible, never to be concealed? In many instances one special sin breeds more distress than a thousand others. That crime has left a deeper scar than any other. In vain you cry, "Out, hideous spot!" Should you wash that hand, it would incarnadine ten thousand Atlantics, and yet it would remain a scarlet spot, never to be erased for ever. No process known to men can wash out the stain. But God's infinite mercy can put away that hideous, unmentionable crime, and it shall be as though it had never been. Possibly, however, you do not so much remember any one transgression as the whole heap of them. Certainly, a multiplicity of minor sins heaped together tower upward like a great Alp, although no one offence may seem so notable as to demand mention. We have sinned every day, and every hour, and almost every moment of every hour: how numberless our transgressions! Our sins of omission are beyond all compute. But all these, too many for you to remember, too many for me to number, are forgiven to the man in Christ: "Having forgiven you all trespasses"—*all*, not one excepted. Thou hast sins not yet known and confessed—but they are forgiven; for the blood cleanseth from all sin.

I should like to help your memory by reminding you of your sins before conversion. Blessed is he whose sin is covered. One does not wish to uncover it. "Lord, remember not the sins of my youth, nor my transgressions." The child of God, who has long been rejoicing in faith, has need still to pray *that;* for our sins may vex our bones long after they have been removed from our consciences: the consequences of a sin may fret us after the sin itself is forgiven.

Then think of your sins after conviction. You were struck down on a certain day with a great sense of sin, and you hurried home and cried upon your knees, "O God, forgive me!" Then you vowed you would never do the like again; but you did. The dog returned to his vomit. You began to attend a place of worship, you were very diligent in religious duties; but on a sudden you went back to your old companions, and your old ways. If your sin was drink, you thought you had mastered it, and could be very moderate; but a fierce thirst came upon you, which you could not resist, and you were soon as drunken as ever. Remember this with shame. Or it may have been a more deliberate backsliding; and deliberation greatly adds to the sin of sins. Without being particularly tempted, you began to hanker after your old pleasures, and almost to despise yourself for having denied yourself their indulgence. I know a man who was present at a prayer-meeting and was so wrought upon that he prayed; but afterwards he said that he would never go into such a place again, for fear he should again be overcome. Think of being afraid to be led aright: ashamed to go to heaven! Ah friends, we have been bullocks unaccustomed to the yoke, dogs that have slipped their collars, horses that have kicked over the traces. Sins after conviction, as doing despite to divine love, are very grievous trespasses. Like the moth, you had your wings singed in the candle, and yet you flew back to the flame: if you had perished in it, who could have pitied you? Yet, after such folly, the Lord had mercy on you: "Having forgiven you all trespasses."

A still worse set of sins must be remembered, sins after conversion, sins after you have found peace with God, after you have enjoyed high fellowship with Jesus. O brothers and sisters, these are cruel wounds for our Lord! These are evils which should melt us to tears even to hear of them. What! pardoned and then sin again! Beloved of the Lord, and still rebelling! You sang so sweetly,

"Thy will be done; thy will be done;"

and then went home and murmured! You talked to others about evil temper, and yet grew angry. You are old and experienced, and yet no boy could have been more imprudent! O God, we bless thee for the morning and the evening lamb; for thy people need the sacrifice perpetually! We need a morning sacrifice, lest the night have gathered aught of evil; and we require an evening sacrifice for the sins of the day.

Dwell for a while upon the large blessing of the text. Whatever your sins may have been, if you are a believer in the Lord Jesus Christ, God has quickened you together with him, and has forgiven you all trespasses. *He pardons most effectually.* Ask God about your sins, and he says, "Their sins and their iniquities will I remember no more!" If God himself does not remember them, they are most effectually removed. Ask Holy Scripture where they are, and Hezekiah tells you, "Thou hast cast all my sins behind thy back." Where is that? God sees everything and everywhere, and therefore everywhere is before his face; if, therefore, he casts our sins behind his back, he throws our sins into "the nowhere": they cease to exist. "In those days, saith the Lord, the iniquity of Israel shall be sought for, and there shall be none; and the sins of Judah, and they shall not be found." Surely this is enough to set all the bells of your heart a-ringing.

Remember, also, dear friends, that *this pardon is most perfect.* He does not commute the punishment, but he pardons the crime. He does not pardon and then confine for life, nor pardon to-day and punish to-morrow: this were not worthy of a God. The pardon is given, and never revoked: the deed of grace is done, and it can never be undone. God will not remember the sin which he has blotted out, nor condemn the offender whom he has absolved. O believer, the Lord so fully absolves thee, that all thy sin, which might have shut thee out of heaven, shall not even hinder thy way thither! All that sin of thine, which might have filled thee with despair, shall not even fill thee with dismay. The Lord shall wipe the tear from thine eyes, as he has washed the sin from thy person. Even the very stain of sin shall be removed. Remember what he says of scarlet and crimson sins. Does he say, "I will wash them so that nothing shall remain beyond a pale red"? Does he say, "I will wash them till nothing shall remain but a slight rosy tint"? No; he says, "They shall be as wool: I will make them white as snow." The Almighty Lord will do his work of remission in an absolutely perfect style, and not a shadow of a spot shall remain.

Here is a point that I must dwell upon for a moment, namely, that *this pardon shall be seen to be perfectly consistent with justice.* If I were pardoned, and felt that God had weakened the foundations of his moral government by winking at evil, I should feel insecure in my pardoned state, and should have no rest. If the justice of God were in the least infringed by my forgiveness, I should feel like a felon towards the universe, and a robber of God. But I bless God that he pardons sin in strict connection with justice. Behold the costly system by which this was effected. He himself came hither in the person of his dear Son; he himself became man, and dwelt among us; he himself took the load of his people's sin; he bare the sin of many, and was made a curse for us. He put away both sin and the curse by his wondrous sacrifice. The marvel of heaven and earth, of time and eternity, is the atoning death of Jesus Christ. This is the mystery that brings more glory to God than all creation, and all providence. How could it be that he should be slain for sinners, the just for the unjust, to bring us to God? To finish transgression, and make an end of sin, was a labour worthy of his Godhead, and Christ has perfectly achieved it by his sufferings and death. You had no fiction before you when, just now, you sang concerning him,

> " Jesus was punish'd in my stead,
> Without the gate my Surety bled
>   To expiate my stain :
> On earth the Godhead deign'd to dwell,
> And made of infinite avail
>   The sufferings of the man."

Now are we justly forgiven; and the throne of God is established. By his death as our Substitute our Lord Jesus has set forth the righteous severity of God as well as his boundless mercy. To us justice and mercy seemed opposed, but in Jesus we see them blended. We bless the Lord for his atoning sacrifice, and feel an infinite satisfaction in the fact that none can dispute the validity of a pardon which comes to us signed by the hand of the eternal King, and counter-signed by the pierced hand of him who bare our sins in his own body on the tree, and gave for those sins a complete vindication of the law which we had broken.

Note well the last consideration upon this point of the forgiveness of all trespasses. It ought to make you feel unutterably happy. Henceforth, *your pardon is bound up with the glory of Christ.* If your pardon does not save you, then Christ is no Saviour. If, resting in him, your sin is not forgiven, then he undertook a fruitless errand when he came to save his people from their sins. Every drop of Christ's blood demands the eternal salvation of every soul that is washed in it. The Godhead and manhood of Christ, and all the glory of his mediatorship, stand up and claim for every believer that he shall be delivered from sin. What! did he bear sin, and shall *we* bear it? Nay : if the Lord hath found in him a ransom, his redeemed are free. Since to save me, who was once dead in sin and in the uncircumcision of my flesh, has become the glory of Christ, I am sure I shall be saved, for he will not tarnish his own name. O believer, to bring you home without spot, or wrinkle, or any such thing, has become the ambition of your Saviour, and he will not fail, or be discouraged. He will neither lose his life-work, nor his death throes. God forbid! And yet this must be, unless you who are quickened together with him, shall be found at the last without fault before the throne of God.

New, let us just think of this: *we are forgiven.* I do not mean all of you; for if you are out of Christ, you have no part in this grand absolution. May the Lord have mercy upon you, quicken you to-day and bring you to Christ! But as many as are trusting in Christ, and so are living in union with him, *you are forgiven.* A person who has been condemned by the law, and then has received a free pardon, walks out of the prison, and goes where he pleases. There is a policeman. Does he fear him? No, he has a free pardon, and the policeman cannot touch him. But there are a great many persons who know him, and know him to be guilty. That does not matter; he has a free pardon, and nobody can touch him. He cannot be tried again, however guilty he may have been; the free pardon has wiped the past right out. Now, to-day, child of God, thou beginnest anew; thou art clean, for he has washed thee, and has done the work right well. We have washed our robes and made them white in the blood of the Lamb, therefore shall we be before the throne of God and praise him. What could we do less than praise him day and night? When shall we ever stop? When we are in his temple, free from all danger of future sin and trial, we will for ever praise him who hath forgiven us all trespasses. I charge you, let us meet in heaven, all of us. Some have dropped in here this morning from all parts of the country, and from America, and we may never meet again on earth. Let us meet around the throne in heaven, and sing "unto him that loved us, and washed us from our sins in his own blood." God grant that we may. Who wants to be left out? Is there one person here who would like to be shut out in that day? I pray you, enter in at once.

> " Come guilty souls, and flee away
> Like doves to Jesus' wounds;
> This is the welcome gospel-day,
> Wherein free grace abounds."

Lydia, the
First European Convert

"And a certain woman named Lydia, a seller of purple, of the city of Thyatira, which worshipped God, heard us: whose heart the Lord opened, that she attended unto the things which were spoken of Paul."—Acts xvi. 14.

WE may laudably exercise curiosity with regard to the first proclamation of the gospel in our own quarter of the globe. We are happy that history so accurately tells us, by the pen of Luke, when first the gospel was preached in Europe, and by whom, and who was the first convert brought by that preaching to the Saviour's feet. I half envy Lydia that she should be the leader of the European band; yet I feel right glad that a woman led the van, and that her household followed so closely in the rear.

God has made great use of women, and greatly honoured them in the kingdom of our Lord and Saviour Jesus Christ. Holy women ministered to our Lord when he was upon the earth, and since that time much sacred work has been done by their patient hands. Man and woman fell together; together they must rise. After the resurrection, it was a woman who was first commissioned to carry the glad tidings of the risen Christ; and in Europe, where woman was in future days to be set free from many of the trammels of the East, it seems fitting that a woman should be the first believer. Not only, however, was Lydia a sort of first-fruit for Europe, but she probably also became a witness in her own city of Thyatira, in Asia. We do not know how the gospel was introduced into that city; but we are informed of the existence of a church there by the message of the ascended Christ, through his servant John, to "the angel of the church in Thyatira." Very likely Lydia became the herald of the gospel in her native place. Let the women who know the truth proclaim it; for why should their influence be lost? "The Lord giveth the word; the women that publish the tidings are a great host." Woman can be as powerful for evil as for good: we see it in this very church of Thyatira, where the woman Jezebel, who called herself a prophetess, sought to seduce many from the truth. Seeing, then, that the devil employs women in his service, let those women whom God has called by his grace be doubly earnest in seeking to prevent or undo the mischief that others of their sex are working. If not called to public service, all have the home-sphere wherein they can shed forth the aroma of a godly life and testimony.

If the gospel does not influence our homes, it is little likely to make headway amongst the community. God has made family piety to be, as it were, a sort of trade-mark on religion in Europe; for the very first convert brings with her all her family. Her household believed, and were baptized with her. You shall notice in Europe, though I do not mean to say that it is not the same anywhere else, that true godliness has always flourished in proportion as family religion has been observed. They hang a bell in a steeple, and they tell us that it is our duty to go every morning and every evening into the steeple-house there to join in prayer; but we reply that our own house is better for many reasons; at any rate, it will not engender superstition for us to pray there. Gather your children together, and offer prayer and supplication to God in your own room.

"But there is no priest." Then there ought to be. Every man should be a priest in his own household; and, in the absence of a godly father, the mother should lead the devotions. Every house should be the house of God, and there should be a church in every house; and when this is the case, it will be the greatest barrier against priestcraft, and the idolatry of holy places. Family prayer and the pulpit are the bulwarks of Protestantism. Depend upon it, when family piety goes down, the life of godliness will become very low. In Europe, at any rate, seeing that the Christian faith began with a converted household, we ought to seek after the conversion of all our families, and to maintain within our houses the good and holy practice of family worship.

Lydia, then, is the first European convert, and we will review her history so far as we have it in Holy Writ. Towards her conversion four things co-operated, upon which we will speak briefly. First, *the working of providence;* secondly, *the working of Lydia herself;* thirdly, *the working of Paul;* and fourthly, *the working of the Holy Spirit.*

I. First, notice THE WORKING OF PROVIDENCE. When I was in Amsterdam, I visited the works of a diamond-cutter, where I saw many large wheels and much powerful machinery at work; and I must confess that it seemed very odd that all that great array of apparatus should be brought to bear upon a tiny bit of crystal, which looked like a fragment of glass. Was that diamond worth so much that a whole factory should be set to work to cut its facets, and cause it to sparkle? So the diamond-cutter believed. Within that small space lay a gem which was thought worthy of all this care and labour. That diamond may be at this time glistening upon the finger or brow of royalty! Now, when I look abroad upon providence, it seems preposterous to believe that kingdoms, dynasties, and great events should all be co-operating and working together for the accomplishment of the divine purpose in the salvation of God's people. But they are so working. It might have seemed preposterous, but it was not so, that these great wheels should all be working for the cutting of a single

116

diamond; and it is not preposterous, however it may seem so, to say that all the events of providence are being ordered by God to effect the salvation of his own people, the perfecting of the precious jewels which are to adorn the crown of Christ for ever and ever.

In the case before us, the working of God's providence is seen, first of all, *in bringing Paul to Philippi*. Lydia is there. I do not know how long she had been there, nor exactly what brought her there; but there she is, selling her purple, her Turkey-red cloth. Paul must come there, too, but he does not want to come; he has not, indeed, had any desire to come there. He has a kind of prejudice hanging about him still, so that, though he is willing to preach to the Gentiles, he scarcely likes to go out of Asia among those Gentiles of the Gentiles over in Europe. He wants to preach the word in Asia. Very singularly, the Spirit suffers him not, and he seems to have a cold hand laid on him to stop him when his heart is warmest. He is gagged; he cannot speak. "Then I will go into Bithynia," he says; but when he starts on the journey, he is distinctly told that there is no work for him to do there. He must not speak for his Master in that region, at least not yet: "the Spirit suffered him not." He feels himself to be a silenced man. What is he to do? He gets down to Troas on the verge of the sea, and there comes to him the vision of a man of Macedonia, who prayed him, saying, "Come over into Macedonia, and help us." He infers that he must go across to Macedonia. A ship is ready for him; he has a free course, a favourable passage, and he soon arrives at Philippi. God brings Paul to the spot where Lydia was, in this strange and singular manner.

But the working of providence was quite as much manifested *in bringing Lydia there;* for Lydia was not originally at Philippi. She was a seller of purple, of Thyatira. Thyatira was a city famous for its dyers. They made a peculiar purple, which was much prized by the Romans. Lydia appears to have carried on this business. She was either a widow, or perhaps had had no husband, though she may have gathered a household of servants about her. She comes over to Philippi across the sea. I think I see them bringing the great rolls of red cloth up the hill, that she may sell at Philippi the cloth which she has made and dyed at Thyatira. Why does she come just at this season? Why does she come just when Paul is coming? Why does she come to Philippi? Why not to Neapolis? Why not press on to Athens? Why not sell her cloth over at Corinth? Whatever reason she might have given for her choice, there was one cause, of which she was ignorant, which shaped her action, and brought her to Philippi at that time. God had a surprise in store for her. She and Paul have to meet. It does not matter what their will is; their wills shall be so moved and actuated by the providence of God that they shall cross each other's path, and Paul shall preach the gospel to Lydia. I wot it never entered into Lydia's heart, when she left Thyatira with her purple bales, that she was going to find Jesus Christ over at Philippi; neither did Paul guess, when he saw, in a vision, a man of Macedonia, and heard him say, "Come over into Macedonia, and help us," that the first person he would have to help would not be a man of Macedonia at all, but a woman of Thyatira; and that the congregation he should preach to would be just a handful of women gathered by the side of the little stream that runs through Philippi. Neither Paul nor Lydia knew what God was about to do; but God knew. He understands the end from the beginning, and times his acts of providence to meet our deepest needs in the wisest way.

> " His wisdom is sublime,
> His heart profoundly kind ;
> God never is before his time,
> And never is behind."

What an odd thing it seemed that this woman should be a woman of Thyatira in Asia, and Paul must not go and preach in Asia ; and yet, when he comes to Macedonia, the first person who hears him is a woman of Asia ! Why, you and I would have said, "If the woman belongs to Thyatira, let her stop at home, and let Paul go there ; that is the shortest cut." Not so. The woman of Thyatira must go to Philippi, and Paul must go to Philippi too. This is God's plan ; and if we knew all the circumstances as God knows them, we should doubtless admire the wisdom of it. Perhaps the very peculiarity of the circumstances made Paul more alert to seize the opportunity at Philippi than he would have been had he gone on to Thyatira ; perhaps the isolation of the strange city made Lydia yearn more after spiritual things. God can answer a dozen ends by one act. One of our evangelists tells of a man who was converted in a small Irish town, and it was afterwards discovered that he, and the preacher who led him to Christ, resided but a few hundred yards from each other in London. They had never met in this great city, where neighbours are strangers to each other ; nor was it likely that they ever would have been brought into contact with one another here ; for the man, who was a commercial traveller, was too careless ever to attend a place of worship in London. But to sell his goods he went to Ireland, where, also, went the evangelist to preach the gospel ; and being somewhat at a loss to know what to do with his time, he no sooner saw the name of a preacher from London announced, than he determined to attend the service, and there he met with Christ. We can see how natural this was in the case of which we know all the particulars, and it was doubtless as well arranged in the case of Lydia and Paul.

Now, I should not wonder to-night if there are a number of providences that have worked together to bring some of my hearers into their places at this time. What brought *you* to London, friend ? It was not your intention to be in this city. Coming to London, what brought you to this part of it ? What led you to be at this service ? And why was it that you did not come on one of the Sundays when the preacher would have been here if he could, but could not be here by reason of his weakness ? Because, it may be, that only from these lips can the word come to you, and only to-night, and you must come to this place. Perhaps there is some one who preaches the gospel much better in the town where you live ; or, peradventure, you have had opportunities of hearing the same preacher near your own door, and you did not avail yourself of them ; and yet God has brought you here. I wish we watched providences more. " Whoso is wise, and will observe these things, even they shall understand the lovingkindness of the Lord." If the Lord should meet with you, and convert you to-night, I will warrant you that you will be a believer in providence, and say, " Yes, God guided my steps. He directed my path, and he brought me to the spot where Jesus met with me, and opened my heart that I might receive the gospel of his grace." Be of good courage, you ministers of the gospel! Providence is always working with you while you are working for God. I have often admired the language of Mahomet, when in the battle of Ohod he said to his followers, pointing to their foes, "Charge them! I can hear the wings of the angels as they hasten to our help." That was a delusion on his part, for he and his men were badly beaten; but it is no delusion in the case of the servants of Christ. We *can* hear the wings of the angels. We may hear the grinding of the great wheels of providence as they revolve for the help of the preacher of the gospel. Everything is with us when we are with God. Who can be against us? The stars in their courses fight for the servants of God; and all things, great and small, shall bow before the feet of him who trod the waves of the Sea of Galilee, and still is Master of all things, and ruleth all things to the accomplishment of his divine purposes.

So much, then, for the working of providence.

II. The next thing is, THE WORKING OF LYDIA. God's intention is that Lydia shall be saved. Yet, you know, no woman was ever saved against her will. God makes us willing in the day of his power, and it is the way of his grace not to violate the will, but sweetly to overcome it. Never will there be anybody dragged to heaven by the ears : depend upon that. We shall go there with all our hearts and all our desires. What, then, was Lydia doing?

Having by God's grace been made willing, the first thing was that *she kept the Sabbath*. She was a proselyte, and she kept the seventh day. She was away from Thyatira, and nobody would know what she would do, yet she observed the Lord's-day carefully. She was abroad when she was at Philippi, but she had not left God behind her. I have known some English people, when they once reached the Continent, go rattling along, Sundays and week-days, as if God did not live on the Continent, and as if at home they only observed the Sabbath because they happened to be in England, which is very probably the case with a good many. When they get away they say, " When you are at Rome, you must do as Rome does ; " and so they take their pleasure on God's day. It was not so with Lydia. There was no selling of purple that day ; she regarded the Sabbath. Oh, I would to God that every one would regard the Sabbath! May God grant that it may never be taken away from us! There is a plot now to make some of you work all the seven days of the week, and you will not get any more pay for seven days than you get for six. Stand out against it, and preserve your right to rest upon God's day. The observance of one day in seven as a day of rest materially helps towards the conversion of men, because then they are inclined to think. They have the opportunity to hear, and, if they choose to avail themselves of it, the probabilities are that God will bless the hearing, and they will be saved.

Now, notice next that, not only did Lydia observe the Sabbath, but *she went up to the place of worship.* It was not a very fine place. I do not suppose there was any building. It may have been a little temporary oratory put up by the river side; but very probably it was just on the bank of the river that they met together. It does not appear that there were any men, but only a few women. They only held a prayer-meeting: "where prayer was wont to be made." But Lydia did not stop away from the gathering. She might easily have excused herself after her long journey, and the wearying work of setting up a new establishment; but her heart was in this matter, and so she found it no drudgery to meet where prayer was offered. She did not say, "I can read a sermon at home," or, "I can read in the Book of the Law indoors." She wished to be where God's people were, however few, or however poor they might be. She did not go to the gorgeous heathen temple at Philippi, but she sought out the few faithful ones that met to worship the true God. Now, dear friends, do the same. You that are not converted, still attend the means of grace, and do not go to a place simply because it is a fine building, and because there is a crowd, but go where they are truly worshipping God in spirit and in truth. If they should happen to be very few and very poor, yet go with them, for in so doing you are in the way of blessing. I think you will yet have to say, "Being in the way, God met with me." If it is what some call "only a prayer-meeting", you will do well to go. Some of the best blessings that men have ever gained have been received at prayer-meetings. If we would meet with God, let us seek him diligently, "not forsaking the assembling of ourselves together, as the manner of some is." Though you cannot save yourself, or open your own heart, you can at least do what Lydia did: observe the Sabbath, and gather together with God's people.

Lydia being there with the assembly, when Paul began to speak, we find that *she attended to the things that were spoken,* which is another thing that we can do. It is very ill when people come up to the house of God, and do not attend. I have never had to complain of people not attending in this house since the day I first preached in it; but I have been in places of worship where there seemed to be anything but attention. How can it be expected that there will be a blessing when the pew becomes a place to slumber in, or when the mind is active over the farm, or in the kitchen, or in the shop, forgetting altogether the gospel which is being preached to the outward ear? If you want a blessing, attend with all your might to the word that is preached; but of that we will speak more by-and-by.

So far we have spoken upon the working of providence and the working of Lydia.

III. Now, next, THE WORKING OF PAUL; for this was necessary too. In order to the conversion of men, it is necessary that the person who aims at their conversion should work as if it all depended upon him, though he knows that he cannot accomplish the work. We are to seek to win souls with as much earnestness, and prudence, and zeal, as if everything depended upon ourselves; and then we are to leave all with God, knowing that none but the Lord can save a single soul.

Now, notice, Paul, wishing for converts, is *judicious in the choice of the place* where he will go to look after them. He goes to the spot

BIBLE STUDY ISSUES

●①●

Nature and shape of the earth: Matthew 4:8
Persons unclean or unholy: Deut. 23:1-2
Offerings respected by God: 2 Samuel 21:
    1-9, Lev. 27:29, Judges 11:30 & 39
Superstition? Isaiah 7:15
Slavery: Lev. 25:44-46, Exodus 21:20 & 21
Equality of women in God's eyes: 1
    Corinthians 14:34, 1 Timothy 2:12
Consistency in facts & figures:
    2 Samuel 10:18, 1 Chronicles 19:18;
    2 Chronicles 9:25, 1 Kings 4:26;
    2 Samuel 8:4, 1 Chronicles 18:4;
    2 Kings 8:26, 2 Chronicles 22:2 & 42
So-called self contradictions:
    Genesis 9:3 and Deuteronomy 14:7-19,
    Deuteronomy 24:16 and Ezekial 18:20
    with the doctrine of Original Sin

INFORMATION UNLIMITED · Box 30544 · Santa Barbara, CA 93130

where there should be a synagogue. He thinks that where people have a desire to pray, there he will find the kind of people who will be ready to hear the word. So he selects devout people, devout worshippers of the one God, that he may go and speak to them about Christ. It is sometimes our plain duty to publish the word from the housetop to the careless crowd; but I think you will generally find that more success comes when those, on whose hearts the Spirit of God has already begun to work, are sought out and instructed. When Christ sent out his disciples on their first journey, he told them, when they entered a town, to "Enquire who in it is worthy; and there abide till ye go thence;" evidently showing that, even amongst those who do not know the truth, there are some whose hearts are prepared to receive it, who are of a devout spirit, and in that sense are worthy. These are the people who should first be sought after. In the same limited sense was Cornelius, to whom Peter was sent, worthy to hear the glad tidings of great joy. His reverent spirit was well pleasing to God; for we read, "Thy prayer is heard, and thine alms are had in remembrance in the sight of God." We must not, of course, think that these things give any claim to salvation; but rather that they are the expression of hearts prepared to receive the message of salvation, seeking the Lord, "if haply they might feel after him, and find him." One of our greatest difficulties in these days is, that so many have lost all reverence for authority of any kind, even God's: having risen against human despotism, they also foolishly try to break God's bands asunder. We are cast back on the infinite power of God when we come to deal with such people; but when we meet with others who are willing to listen and pray, we know that God has already begun to work. Now, dear worker, choose the person who is evidently pointed out to you by God's gracious providence. Choose judiciously, and try to speak with those with whom you may hopefully speak, and trust that God will bless the word.

When Paul goes down to the river, you notice that he is very *judicious as to his manner* of introducing his subject. He did not preach at all. He found only a few women; and to stand up and preach to them, as he did to the crowds at Corinth, or at Athens, might have seemed absurd; but we read this: "We sat down, and spake unto the women which resorted thither." He took his seat on the river's bank, where they were all sitting still, and at prayer, and he began just to have a talk. A sermon would have been out of place; but a talk was the right sort of thing. So he talked the gospel into them. Now, be careful of the way in which you go to work with people; for much of the result must depend upon that. Some people can be preached right away from Christ; for the moment you begin to preach they say, "Oh, thank you, I do not want any of your sermon!" Perhaps you could slip a word in edgewise; just drop a seed in a crack; or leave a word with them, just one word. Say at once, "If you do not want any preaching, I do not want to preach to you: I am not so fond of preaching as all that; but I read a very curious story in the newspapers the other day!" And then tell the story, and wrap the gospel up in it. If they do not want pills, do not give them pills. Give them a bit of sugar. They will take the sugar, and when they get it, there will be a pill inside. I mention this, because we may miss opportunities of doing good through not being wide awake. "Be ye wise as serpents, and harmless as doves." Paul therefore just sits down, and has a friendly talk with the women who resorted thither.

But whether Paul preached, or whether Paul talked, it was all the same: he was *judicious as to the matter* of his discourse. He had but one subject, and that was Christ; the Christ who had met him on the way to Damascus, and changed his heart; the Christ who was able still to save; the Christ who bled upon the cross, to bring men to God, and cleanse them in his blood; the Christ in heaven, interceding for sinners; the Christ waiting to be gracious. Paul would not end his talk without saying, "Trust him: trust him. He that believeth in him hath everlasting life." So, whether he preached or whether he talked, it was the same story of Jesus Christ, and him crucified. That is how Paul worked. He might have acted very differently. If his heart had not been all aflame for Jesus, he would very likely not have spoken at all, or if he had, it would have been a commonplace remark about the weather. He might have been eager to learn the method by which the beautiful purple dye was obtained, and not have remembered that gospel message, written by Isaiah long ago, which would come with special force to the hearts of his hearers: " Though your sins be as scarlet, they shall be as white as snow; though they be red like crimson, they shall be as wool." He might have been so interested in his enquiries about Thyatira as to forget to speak of the way to the city of light. A dozen subjects might have claimed attention, if his heart had not been set upon one object. He could have spoken of his journeys, and even of his plans, without actually preaching Christ to her. He might have spoken about the gospel, as I fear we often do, and not have spoken the gospel itself. Some sermons which I have heard, though faultlessly orthodox, have contained nothing that could convert anybody; for there has been nothing to touch the conscience or heart. Others, though very clever and profound, have had no possible bearing on the needs of the hearers; and so it was little wonder that they were without result. But I am sure Paul's talk would aim straight at the centre of the target: it was evidently addressed to the heart; for we are told that it was with the heart Lydia heard it. After all, it is not our most orderly discourses, nor our aptest illustrations, which bring people to Christ; but some little sentence which is slipped in unawares, or some burning word which comes straight out of our own heart's experience. There would be sure to be many such that day in that earnest simple talk by the river side. Let us multiply such conversations, if we would win more Lydias for the church.

IV. But, now, fourthly—and here is the main point—let us notice THE WORKING OF THE SPIRIT OF GOD. Providence brings Paul and Lydia together. Lydia comes there because she observes the Sabbath, and loves the place of worship. Paul comes there because he loves to win souls, and, like his Master, is on the watch for stray sheep. But it would have been a poor meeting for them if the Spirit of God had not been there also. So we next read of Lydia: " Whose heart the Lord opened, that she attended unto the things which were spoken of Paul."

It is not wonderful that the Lord can open a human heart; for he who made the lock knows well what key will fit it. What means he made use of in the case of Lydia, I do not know; but I will tell you what might have happened. Perhaps she had lost her husband; many a woman's heart has been opened by that great gash. The joy of her soul has been taken away, and she has turned to God. Perhaps her husband was spared to her; but she had lost a child. Oh, how many a babe has been sent here on purpose to entice its mother to the skies; a lamb taken away that the sheep might follow the Shepherd! Perhaps she had had bad trade; the price of purple may have fallen. She may have been half afraid she would fail in business. I have known such trouble open some people's hearts. Perhaps she had had prosperity; possibly the purple had gone up in price. I have known some so impressed with God's temporal blessings that they have been ready to think of him, and to turn to him. I do not know; I cannot guess, and I have no right to guess what it was. But I know that God has very wonderful ploughs, with which he breaks up the hard soil of human hearts. When I have been through the Britannia Iron Works, at Bedford, I have wondered at the strange clod-crushers, clod-breakers, and ploughs, made there by the Messrs. Howard; and God has some marvellous machines in his providence for turning up the soil of our hearts. I cannot tell what he has done to you, dear friend, but I do trust that whatever has happened has been opening the soil, so that the good seed may drop in. It was the Spirit of God who did it, whatever the instrument may have been, and Lydia's heart was "opened." Opened to what? To attend. "She attended unto the things which were spoken of Paul."

So, first, her heart was opened *to listen very intently.* She wanted to catch every word. She did as some of you do, put her hand to her ear, for fear she should not hear all that was spoken. There are many ways of listening. Some people listen with both their ears, allowing it to go in at one ear and out at the other; like that wit, who, when he was being seriously spoken to, and yet seemed very inattentive, at length wearied the friend who was discoursing. "I am afraid it is not doing you much good," he said. "No," came the reply; "but I think it will do this gentleman some good," pointing to one who sat beside him, "for as it has gone in at this side it has gone out at the other." Oh, how I wish that you had only one ear, so that the truth you hear could never get out again after it had once got in! Well did the Lord speak through Isaiah the prophet unto the people, "Hearken *diligently* unto me, and eat ye that which is good." Many people can listen for an hour or two to a scientific lecture, or a political speech, without feeling in the least weary; they can even go to the theatre, and sit there a whole evening without dreaming of being tired; yet they complain if the sermon is a minute beyond the appointed time. They seem to endure the preaching as a sort of penance, scarcely hearing the words, or, at least, never imagining that the message can have any application to their own case.

Lydia's heart was so opened "that she attended", that is, she listened to the word of salvation until she began *to desire it.* It is always a pleasure to entertain guests who relish the food placed before them; and it is a great joy to preach to those who are eagerly hungering after the truth. But how heart-breaking a task it is to keep continually praising the pearl of great price to those who know not its value, nor desire its beauty! Daniel was a man "greatly beloved"; the Hebrew word there employed means "a man of desires." He was not one of your conceited, self-satisfied individuals. He longed and yearned for better things than he had yet attained, and hence was "greatly beloved." God loves people to thirst after him, and to desire to know his love and power. Let us explain the gospel as we may, if there is no desire in the heart, our plainest messages are lost. A man said, about something he wished to make clear, "Why, it is as plain as A B C!" "Yes," said a third party, "but the man you are talking to is D E F." So, some of our hearers seem to turn away from the Word of God. But when a person says, "I want to find salvation; I want to get Christ this very day; and I am going to listen with the determination that I will find out the way of salvation;" surely, if the things spoken are the same things that Paul spoke of, few in that condition will go out of the house without finding salvation. Lydia's heart was opened to attend to the gospel, that is, to desire it.

But, next, her heart was opened *to understand it*. It is wonderful how little even well-educated people sometimes understand of the gospel when it is preached in the simplest manner. One is constantly being astounded by the misapprehensions that persons have as to the way of salvation. But Lydia had grasped the truth. "Thanks be to God," she said, "I see it. Jesus Christ suffered in our stead; and we, by an act of faith, accept him as our Substitute, and we are saved thereby. I have it. I never saw it before. I read about a paschal lamb, and the sprinkling of the blood, and the passing over of the houses where the blood was sprinkled. I could not quite make it out. Now I see, if the blood be sprinkled upon me, God will pass over me, according to his word, 'When I see the blood, I will pass over you.'" She attended unto the things which were spoken of Paul, so as to understand them.

But more than that; her heart was so opened that she attended to the gospel so as *to accept it*. "Ah!" she said, "now I understand it, I will have it. Christ for me! Christ for me! That blessed Substitute for sinners! Is that all I have to do, simply to trust him? Then I will trust him. Sink or swim, I will cast myself upon him now." She did so there and then. There was no hesitating. She believed what Paul said; that Jesus was the Son of God, the appointed propitiation for sin, and that whosoever believed on him should then and there be justified; and she did believe in him, and she was justified; as you will be, my friend, if you will believe in him at this moment. You, too, shall have immediate salvation, my dear sister sitting yonder, if you will come, like this Lydia of old, and just take Christ to be yours, and trust him now. She attended unto the things which were spoken of Paul, so that she accepted Christ.

Having done that, she went further: her heart was so won, that she was, by the Spirit, led *to obey the word, and avow her faith*. Paul told her that the gospel was this—"He that believeth and is baptized shall be saved." He said to her, "My commission is, 'Go ye into all the world, and preach the gospel to every creature. He that believeth and is baptized shall be saved.'" Perhaps she said, "But why must I be baptized?" He said, "As a testimony of your obedience to Christ, whom you take to be your Master and your Lord; and as a type of your being one with him in his burial. You are to be buried in water as he was buried in the tomb of Joseph; and you are to be raised up out of the water even as he rose again from the dead. This act is to be a token and type to you of your oneness with him in his death and burial and resurrection." What did Lydia say? Did she say, "Well, I think I must wait a little while: the water is cold"? Did she say, "I think I must ask about it; I must consider it"? No, not at all. Paul tells her that this is Christ's ordinance, and she at once replies, "Here am I, Paul, let me be baptized, and my servants, too, and all that belong to my household, for they also believe in Jesus Christ. Let us have the baptism at once." There and then "she was baptized, and her household." She did at once obey the heavenly message, and she became a baptized believer. She was not ashamed to confess Christ. She had not known him long; but what she did know of him was so blessed and joyous to her soul, that she would have said, if she had known the hymn—

> "Through floods and flames, if Jesus lead,
>   I'll follow where he goes;
> 'Hinder me not,' shall be my cry,
>   Though earth and hell oppose."

You can imagine her saying, "Did he go down into the Jordan, and say, 'Thus it becometh us to fulfil all righteousness'? Then I will go where he leads the way, and be obedient to him, and say to all the world, 'I, too, am a follower of the crucified Christ.'"

Now, lastly, after Lydia was baptized, *she became an enthusiastic Christian.* She said to Paul, "You must come home with me. I know you have not anywhere to go. Come along; and there is your friend Silas. I have plenty of room for him; and Timothy too; and Luke also. We can make room for the four of you among the purple bales, or somewhere; but, at any rate, I have house-room for you four, and I have heart-room for forty thousand of you. I wish I could take in the whole church of God." Dear good woman that she was, she felt that she could not do too much for the men who had been made a blessing to her; for she regarded what she did to them as done to their Lord and Master. They might have said, "No, really, we cannot trouble you. You have the household. You have all this business to look after." "Yes," she would answer, "I know that. It is very kind of you to excuse yourselves; but you must come." "No," Paul might urge, "my dear good woman, I am going to find out some tent-makers, and make tents with them. We will find a lodging where we have been." "Ah!" she would say, "but I mean to have you. You must come to my home." "She constrained us." She would probably put it thus: "Now, I shall not think that you fully believe in me if you do not come home with me. Come, you baptized me, and by that very act you professed that you considered that I was a true believer. If you do really believe it, come and stay in my house as long as you like, and I will make you as comfortable as ever I can." So at last Paul yields to her constraint, and goes to her home. How glad they would all be, and what praise to Christ would rise from that household! I hope that the generous spirit, which glowed in the heart of the first convert in Europe, will always continue amongst the converts of Europe till the last day. I trust that when they are called not merely to entertain God's ministers, but to help all God's people of every sort, they may be ready and willing to do it for Christ's sake; for love shall fill them with a holy hospitality, and an earnest desire to bless the children of God. Love one another, brothers and sisters, and do good to one another, as you have opportunity; for so will you be worthy followers of Lydia, the first European convert, whose heart the Lord opened.

The Lord open your hearts, for his name's sake! Amen.

"Even Now"

"Even now."—John xi. 22.

I HOPE that there are a great many persons here who are interested in the souls of those around them. We shall certainly never exercise faith concerning those for whose salvation we have no care. I trust, also, that we are diligent in looking after individuals, especially those who are amongst our own family and friends. This was what Martha did; her whole care was for her brother. It is often easier to have faith that Christ can save sinners in general, than to believe that he can come into our own home, and save some particular member of our household. But, oh, the joy when this comes to pass; when we are able to kneel beside some of our loved ones, and rejoice with them in being made alive by the power of the Holy Ghost! We cannot expect to have this privilege, however, unless like Martha we send our prayer to Jesus, and go to meet him, and tell him of our need. In the presence of Christ it seems very natural to trust him even at the worst extremity. It is when we are at our wits' end that he delights to help us. When our hopes seem to be buried, then it is that God can give us a resurrection. When our Isaac is on the altar, then the heavens are opened, and the voice of the Eternal is heard. Art thou giving way to despair concerning thy dear friend? Art thou beginning to doubt thy Saviour, and to complain of his delay? Be sure that Jesus will come at the right time, though he must be the judge of which is the best time for him to appear.

Martha had a fine faith. If we all had as much honest belief in Christ as she had, many a man, who now lies dead in his sins, would, ere long, hear that voice which would call him forth from his tomb, and restore him unto his friends. Martha's faith had to do with a dreadful case. Her brother was dead, and had been buried, but her faith still lived; and in spite of all things which went against her, she believed in Christ, and looked to him for help in her extremity. Her faith went to the very edge of the gulf, and she said, " But I know, that *even now*, whatsoever thou wilt ask of God, God will give it thee."

Still, Martha had not so much faith as she thought she had. But a few hours after she had confessed her confidence in the power of the Lord Jesus, or perhaps it was only a few minutes, she stood at the grave of her brother, and evidently doubted the wisdom of him she professed to trust. She objected to the stone being removed; and, strong in the admitted facts of the case, she urged her reason, and said, " Lord, by this time he stinketh." Well, but, Martha, you said, not very long ago, "I know that even now the Christ can interpose." Yes, she said it, and she believed it in the way in which most of us believe ; but when her faith was sharply tried by a matter of fact, she did not appear to have had all the faith she professed. I suspect this also is true of most of us. We often fancy our confidence in Christ is much stronger than it really is. I think I have told you of my old friend, Will Richardson, who said, when he was seventy-five years of age, that it was a very curious thing, that all the winter through, he thought he should like to be a-harvesting, or out in the hay-field, because he felt so strong. He imagined that he could do as much as any of the youngsters. " But," he said, "do you know, Mr. Spurgeon, when the summer comes, I do not get through the hay-making ; and when the autumn comes, I find I have not sufficient strength for reaping ? " So it often is in spiritual things. When we are not called upon to bear the trouble, we feel wonderfully strong ; but when the trial comes, very much of our boasted faith is gone in smoke. Take heed that ye examine well your faith ; let it be true and real, for you will need it all.

However, Christ did not take Martha at her worst, but at her best. When our Lord says, "According to your faith be it unto you," he does not mean "According to your faith in its ebb," but "According to your faith in its flood." He reads the thermometer at its highest point, not at its lowest ; not even taking the "mean temperature" of our trust. He gives us credit for our quickest pace ; not counting our slowest, nor seeking to discover our average speed in this matter of faith. Christ did for Martha all she could have asked or believed ; her brother did rise again, and he was restored to her, and to his friends. In thy case, too, O thou trembling, timorous believer, the Lord Jesus will take thee at thy best, and he will do for thee great things, seeing that thou desirest to believe greatly, and that thy prayer is, " Lord, I believe ; help thou mine unbelief ! "

The point upon which Martha chiefly rested, when she expressed her faith, was the power of Christ in intercession with his Father. "I know," said she, "that, even now, whatsoever thou wilt ask of God, God will give it thee." Since the omnipotence of God could be claimed, she felt no anxiety as to the greatness of the request. " Whatsoever " was asked could easily be gained, if it was only asked by him who never was denied. Beloved in the Lord, our Christ is still alive, and he is still pleading. Can you believe, even now, that whatever he shall ask of God, God will give it him, and give it you for his dear Son's sake ? What an anchorage is the intercession of Christ! " He is able also to save them to the uttermost that come unto God by him, seeing he ever liveth to make intercession for them." Here is a grand pillar to rest the weight of our souls upon : "He ever liveth to make intercession for them." Surely, we may have great faith in him who never wearies, and who never fails; who lives, indeed, for no other purpose than to plead for those who trust in his dying love, and in his living power. "Who is he that condemneth? It is Christ that died, yea, rather, that is risen again, who is even at the right hand of God, who also maketh intercession for us." Fall back upon the intercessory power of Christ in every time of need, and you will find comfort that will never fail you.

It is a grand thing to have faith for the present, not bemoaning the past, nor dreaming of some future faith which we hope may yet be ours. The present hour is the only time we really possess. The past is gone beyond recall. If it has been filled with faith in God, we can no more live on that faith now than we can live to-day on the bread we ate last week. If, on the contrary, the past has been marred by our unbelief, that is no reason why this moment should not witness a grand triumph of trust in the faithful Saviour. Let us not excuse our present lack of faith by the thought of some future blessing. No confidence which we may learn to put in Christ, in the days to come, can atone for our present unbelief. If we ever mean to trust him, why should we not do so now, since he is as worthy of our belief now as he ever will be, and since what we miss now we miss beyond recall.

> " The present, the present is all thou hast
>   For thy sure possessing,
> Like the patriarch's angel, hold it fast,
>   Till it give its blessing."

In this verse, " I know, that even now, whatsoever thou wilt ask of God, God will give it thee," I want to fix your attention only on the two words, " Even now." We have just sung—

> "Pass me not, O tender Saviour,
>   Let me love and cling to thee;
> I am longing for thy favour;
>   When thou comest, call for me:
>   Even me."

Our hymn was, " Even me." The sermon is to be " Even now." If you have been singing " Even me," and so applying the truth to your own case, say also, with an energy of heart that will take no denial, " Even now," and listen with earnest expectation to that gospel which is always in the present tense : " While it is said, To-day if ye will hear his voice, harden not your heart, as in the provocation." Remember, too, that this is not only the preacher's word, for the Holy Ghost saith, " To-day " : " Even now."

I shall use these words, first, in reference *to those who are concerned about the souls of others*, as Martha was about her dead brother. Believe that Christ can save even now. Then I shall speak *to you who are somewhat concerned about your own souls*. You believe, perhaps, that Christ can save. I want you to be persuaded that he can save you even now; that is to say, at this exact hour and minute, going by the clock, while you hear these words, even now, Christ can forgive; even now, Christ can save; even now, Christ can bless.

I. First, CAN WE BELIEVE THIS WITH REFERENCE TO OTHERS? If you are in the same position as Martha, I can bring out several points of likeness which should encourage you to persevere. You, mother, have prayed for your boy; you, father, have pleaded for your girl; you, dear wife, have been much in prayer for your husband; you, beloved teacher, have frequently brought your class before God; and yet there is a bad case now pressing upon your mind, and your heart is heavy about some dear one, whose condition seems hopeless. I want you to believe that now, even now, Christ can grant your prayer, and save that soul; that now, even now, he can give you such a blessing that the past delay shall be more than recompensed to you.

There is one, for instance, in whom we are deeply interested, and we can say that *the case has cost us great sorrow.* So Martha could have said of Lazarus. "Blessed Master", she might have said, "my brother took the fever"—(for I should think it was a fever that he had)—"and I watched him; I brought cold water from the well, and I laved his burning brow; I was by his bedside all night. I never took off my clothes. Nobody knows how my heart was wrung with anguish as I saw the hot beaded drops upon his brow, and tried to moisten his parched tongue and lips. I sorrowed as though I was about to die myself; but in spite of all that, I believe even now that thou canst help me; even now." Alas! there are many griefs in the world like this. A mother says, "Nobody knows what I have suffered through that son of mine. I shall die of a broken heart because of his conduct." "No one can tell," says a father, "what grief that daughter of mine has caused me. I have sometimes wished that she had never been born." There have been many, many such stories told into my ear, in which a beloved one has been the cause of anguish and agony untold to gracious, loving hearts. To those so sorely troubled I now speak. Can you believe that *even now* the living Intercessor is "mighty to save"? It may be that you are at this moment trembling on the verge of the blessing you so long have sought. God give you faith to grasp it "even now"!

With other persons we are met with a fresh difficulty. *The case has already disappointed us.* That is how some of you have found it, is it not? "Yes," you say, "I have prayed long for a dear friend, and I believed, some time ago, that my prayer was heard, and that there was a change for the better; indeed, there was an apparent change; but it came to nothing." You are just like Martha. She kept saying to herself, "Christ will come. Brother is very ill, but Jesus will come before he dies; I know he will. It cannot be that he will stay away much longer; and when he comes, Lazarus will soon be well." Day after day, Mary and she sent their messenger to look toward the Jordan, to see if Jesus was not coming. But he did not come. It must have been a terrible disappointment to both these sisters; enough to stagger the strongest faith they had ever had in the sympathy of Christ. But Martha got the better of it, and she said, "Even now, though disappointed so bitterly, I believe that thou canst do whatsoever thou wilt." Learn from Martha, my discouraged brother. You thought that your friend was converted, but he went back again; you thought that there was a real work of grace upon his heart, but it turned out to be a mere disappointment, and disappeared, like the mist before the sun. But can you not believe over the head of your disappointment, and say, "I believe even now, even now"? Blessed shall your faith be, if it gets so far.

Perhaps further difficulties have met us. We have attempted to help someone, and *the case has proved our own helplessness.* "Ah, yes," says one, "that exactly describes me. I never felt so helpless in my life. I have done all that I can do, and it amounts to nothing. I have been careful in my example. I have been prayerful in my words. I have been very patient and longsuffering. I have tried to induce my beloved one to go and listen to the gospel here and there. I have put holy books in his way, and all the while I have seized opportunities to plead with him, often with tears in my eyes, and I can do nothing! I am dead beat." Yes, that is just where Martha got to; she had done everything, and nothing seemed to be of the least use. None of the medicines she applied seemed to soothe the sufferer. She had gone down the village, perhaps to the house of Simon the leper, who was a friend of hers, and he possibly advised some new remedies; but nothing seemed to make the least difference. Her brother got worse and worse, until she saw that, though she had nursed him back to health the last time he had been ill, she was now utterly powerless. Then he died. Yet, even though things had gone so far as that, she had faith in Christ. In like manner, your case is beyond your skill; but can you not believe that, even now, the end of nature will be the beginning of grace; can you not even now feel that you shall find that word true, "He shall not fail"? Christ never did fail yet, and he never will. When all the doctors give a patient up, the Great Physician can step in and heal. Can you believe concerning your friend "even now"?

But perhaps you are in a worse plight still. *The case has been given up.* I think I hear one kind, gracious soul, whose hope has been crushed, say, "Well, sir, that is just what we have come to about my boy. We held a little family meeting, and said we must get him to go away to Australia, if we can. If he will only go to America, or somewhere abroad, it will be a relief to have him out of our sight. He keeps coming home intoxicated, and gets brought before the magistrates. He is a disgrace to us. He is a shame to the name he bears. We have given him up." Martha had come to this. She had given her brother up, and had actually buried him; yet she believed in the power of Christ. Ah, there are many people that are buried alive! I do not know that such a thing ever happens in the cemetery; but I know it happens in our streets and homes. Many are buried morally, and given up by us before God gives them up. And, somehow, it is often the given-up people that God delights to bless. Can you believe that even now, *even now,* prayer can be heard, that even now the Holy Ghost can change the nature, and that even now Christ can save the soul? Believest thou this? I shall rejoice if thou canst, and thou too shalt rejoice ere long.

But there is still a lower depth. Here is one who is much concerned about an individual, and *the case is loathsome.* "Though we loved him once," he says, " his character has now become such that it is pestilential to the family. He leads others astray. We cannot think of what he has done without the very memory of his life spreading a taint over our conscience, and over our mind." There are persons alive in the world, who are just masses of living putridity. There may be such here. I should be glad if a word I said could reach them. It is a shocking thing that there are men and women, made in the image of God, with talents and ability, with capacity and conscience, who, nevertheless, seem to live for nothing else but to indulge their licentious passions, and to lead others into vices which else they had never known. There must come an awful day of reckoning to such when the Christ of God shall sit upon the throne, and shall weigh before all men the secret doings of libertines, of debauched men, and depraved women. If any of you have such a one related to you, can you believe that even now Christ can raise that one? Yours is just the same sort of case as Martha had. She could have said, " Brother is buried: worse than that, he stinketh." She did not like to say that of dear Lazarus, her own brother, but she could not help saying it. And there are some men, of whom we are compelled to say, no matter how much our love seeks to shield them, that their character stinks. But can you still believe that, even now, there is hope that God can intervene, and that grace can save? Why, my dear friend, you and I know that it is so! I do believe it; we must all believe it. If it comes to a case very near and dear to you, and you begin to be a little bit staggered, recollect what you used to be yourselves—not openly so depraved, perhaps, but inwardly quite the same, and take hope for these foul men and women from the remembrance of what you were: "and such were some of you; but ye are washed." When John Newton used to preach at St. Mary Woolnoth, he always believed in the possibility of the salvation of the worst of his hearers; for he had been himself one of the vilest of the vile. When he was very old, and they said, "Dear Mr. Newton, you are too old to preach; you had better not go into the pulpit now," he said, "What! shall the old African blasphemer, who has been saved by grace, leave off preaching the gospel while there is breath in his body? Never." I think while there is breath in the body of some of us, we must go on telling the gospel; for, if it saved us, it can save the worst of sinners. We are bound to believe that even now Christ can save even the most horrible and the most vile.

> " His blood can make the foulest clean,
> His blood availed for me."

Perhaps there is even a more desperate difficulty still, with reference to someone whom we would fain see living for God. *The case is beyond our reach.* "Yes," that brother quickly answers, " now you have come to my trouble. I do not even know where my boy is; he ran away, and we have not heard from him for years. How can I help him?" Why, believe that " even now " Christ can speak to him, and save him! He can send his grace where we can send our love. The great difficulty which lies like a stone at the door of the sepulchre will not prevent him speaking the life-giving word. He has all forces at his command, and when he says the word, the stone shall be rolled away, and the son that is lost shall be found; the dead shall be made alive again. Though you cannot reach your son, or your daughter, Christ can meet with them. "The Lord's hand is not shortened, that it cannot save; neither his ear heavy, that it cannot hear." Though your prodigal boy or your wandering girl be at the end of the earth, Christ can reach them, and save them. "Have faith in God." "Even now" Christ can aid you.

> " Faith, mighty faith, the promise sees,
> And looks to God alone,
> Laughs at impossibilities,
> And says, 'It shall be done.'"

I know there are some Christian people who have drifted into the terribly wicked state of giving up their relatives as hopeless. There was a brother here, who is now in heaven, a good, earnest Christian man, whose son had treated him very shockingly indeed, and the father, justly indignant, felt it right to give his son up. He had often tried to help him, but the young man was so scandalous a scapegrace that I did not wonder that the old man turned him away. But one night, as I was preaching here, I spoke in something like the same way in which I have spoken now; and the next morning the old man's arm was about his child's neck. He could not help himself; he felt he must go and find his son out, and seek again to reclaim him. It seemed to have been the appointed time for that boy's salvation, for it pleased God that within a few months that son died, and he passed away with a good hope, through grace, that he had been brought to his Saviour's feet by his father's love. If any of you have a very bad son, go after him, seeking, until by the grace of God, you shall find him. And you that have grown hopeless about your relatives, you must try not to give them up. If other people cast them off, you must not, for they are allied to you by the ties of blood. Seek them out. You are the best person in the world to seek them, and the most likely to find them, if you can believe that even now, when the worst has come to the worst, "even now," almighty grace can step in, and save the lost soul.

Oh, that some here may have faith to claim at this moment the salvation of their friends! May desire be wrought into expectancy, and hope become certainty! Like Jacob at Jabbok, may we lay hold of God, saying, "I will not let thee go, except thou bless me ." To such faith the Lord will give a quick response. He that will not be denied shall not be denied. My friend, Hudson Taylor, who has done such a wonderful work for China, is an instance of this. Brought up in a godly home, he, as a young man, tried to imitate the lives of his parents, and failing in his own strength to make himself better, he swung to the other extreme, and began to entertain sceptical notions. One day, when his mother was from home, a great yearning after her boy possessed her, and she went up to her room to plead with God that " even now " he would save him. If I remember aright, she said that she would not leave the room until she had the assurance that her boy would be brought to Christ. At length her faith triumphed, and she rose quite certain that all was well, and that "even now" her son was saved. What was he doing at that time? Having half an hour to spare, he wandered into his father's library, and aimlessly took down one book after another to find some short and interesting passage to divert his mind. He could not find what he wanted in any of the books; so, seeing a narrative tract, he took it up with the intention of reading the story, and putting it down when the sermon part of it began. As he read, he came to the words "the finished work of Christ", and almost at the very moment in which his mother, who was miles away, claimed his soul of God, light came into his heart. He saw that it was by the finished work of Christ that he was to be saved; and kneeling in his father's library, he sought and found the life of God. Some days afterwards, when his mother returned, he said to her, "I have some news to tell you." "Oh, I know what it is!" she answered, smiling, "You have given yourself to God." "Who told you?" he asked, in astonishment. "God told me," she said, and together they praised him, who, at the same moment, gave the faith to the mother, and the life to the son, and who has since made him such a blessing to the world. It was the mother's faith, claiming the blessing "even now", that did it. I tell you this remarkable incident that many others may be stirred up to the same immediate and importunate desire for the salvation of their children and relatives. There are some things we must always pray for with submission as to whether it is the will of God to bestow them upon us: but for the salvation of men and women we may ask without a fear. God delights to save and to bless; and when the faith is given to us to expect an immediate answer to such a prayer, thrice happy are we. Seek such faith even now, I beseech you, "even now."

II. But, in the second place, I want to speak very earnestly to any here who are concerned about their own souls. Jesus can save you "even now." CAN WE BELIEVE THIS FOR OURSELVES? Can you expect the Lord, even while you hear these words, to speak to you the word of power, and bring you forth from your sleep of sin?

For some of you, *the time is late, very late; yet it is not too late.* You are getting into years, my friend. I want you to believe that even now Christ can save you. I often notice the number of old people who come to the Tabernacle. I am glad to see the aged saints; but amongst so many elderly people, no doubt, there are some unsaved sinners, whose grey hairs are not a crown of glory, but a fool's cap. But, however old you are, though you are sixty, seventy, eighty, or even ninety years of age, yet "even now" Christ can give you life. Blessed be God for that! But it is not altogether the years that trouble you; it is your sins. As I have already said, if you have gone to the very extremity of sin, you may believe that, after all these years of wandering, the arms of free grace are still open to receive you "even now." There is an old proverb, "It is never too late to mend." It is ever too late for us to mend ourselves, but it is never too late for Christ to mend us. Christ can make us new, and it is never too late for him to do it. If you come to him, and trust him, he will receive you "even now."

By the longsuffering of God, *there is a time left to you*, in which you may turn to him. What a thousand mercies it is that "even now" is a time of mercy to you: it might have been the moment of your everlasting doom! You have been in accidents; you have been within an inch of the grave many times; you have been ill, seriously ill; you have been well-nigh given up for dead; and here you are yet alive, and still an enemy to God! Plucked by his hand from fire and flood, and, mayhap, from battle; delivered from fever and cholera, and still ungrateful, still rebelling, still spending the life that grace has lent you in resisting the love of God! Long years ago you should have believed in Christ, but the text is "even now." Do not begin to say, "I believe that God could have saved me years ago;" there is no faith in that. Do not meet my earnest plea, by saying, "I believe that God can save me under such-and-such conditions." Believe that he can save you now, up in the top gallery there, just as you are. You came in here careless and thoughtless; yet, even now, he can save you. Away yonder, quite a man of the world, free and easy, destitute of all religious inclinations though you may be, he can save you even now. O God, strike many a man down, as thou didst Saul of Tarsus, and change their hearts by thine own supreme love, as thou canst do it, even now, on the very spot where they sit or stand!

But though God waits to be gracious to you, though you have yet time to repent, remember, *it is but a time, therefore seize it.* Your opportunity will not last for ever. I believe that even now God can save; but if you reject Christ, there will come a time when salvation will be impossible. On earth, as long as a man desires to be saved, he may be saved: while there is life there is hope. I believe that, if a man's breath were going from his body, if he could then look to Christ, he would live. But—

> "There are no acts of pardon passed
> In the cold grave, to which we haste;
> But darkness, death, and long despair,
> Reign in eternal silence there."

Do not venture on that last leap without Christ; but even now, ere the clock strikes another time, fly to Jesus. Trust him "even now."

It is a time of hope. Even now, there is still every opportunity and every preparation for the sinner's salvation. "Behold, now is the accepted time; behold, now is the day of salvation." Shall I give you some reasons for believing that "even now" is a time of hope? There are many good arguments which may be brought forward, in order to banish the thought of despair.

First, *the gospel is still preached*. The old-fashioned gospel is not dead yet. There are a great many who would like to muzzle the mouths of God's ministers; but they never will. The old gospel will live when they are dead; and, because it is still preached to you, you may believe and live. What is the old gospel? It is that, seeing you are helpless to save yourself, or bring yourself back to God, Christ came to restore you; that he took those sins of yours, which were enough to sink you to hell, and bore them on the cross, that he might bring you to heaven. If you will but trust him, even now, he will deliver you from the curse of the law; for it is written, "He that believeth on him is not condemned." If you will trust him, even now, he will give you a life of blessedness, which will never end; for again it is written, "He that believeth on the Son hath everlasting life." Because that gospel is preached, there is hope for you. When there is no hope, there will be no presentation of the gospel. God must, by an edict, suspend the preaching of the gospel ere he can suspend the fulfilment of the gospel promise to every soul that believeth. Since there is a gospel, take it; take it now, even now. God help you so to do!

In the second place, I know there is hope now, "even now"; for *the Christ still lives.* He rose from the dead, no more to die, and he is as strong as ever. "I am he that liveth and was dead," he saith, "and behold, I am alive for evermore. Amen." Those words were spoken to the Apostle John, and when he saw him, he said that "His head and his hairs were white like wool, as white as snow;" but when the spouse saw him, she said, "His locks are bushy, and black as a raven." Yet both saw truly; John's vision of the white hair was to show that Christ is the Ancient of Days; but the view of the spouse was to show his everlasting youth, his unceasing strength and power to save. If there is any difference in him, Christ is to-day more mighty to save than he was when Martha saw him. He had not then completed the work of our salvation, but he has perfectly accomplished it now; and therefore there is hope for everyone who trusts in him. My Lord has gone up yonder where a prayer will find him, with the keys of death and hell jingling at his girdle, and with the omnipotence of God in his right hand. If you believe on him, by his "eternal power and Godhead" he will save you, and save you even now, on the spot, before you leave this house.

Moreover, I know that this is a time of hope, in the next place, because *the precious blood still has power.* All salvation is through the blood of the Lamb. Still—

> " There is a fountain filled with blood,
> Drawn from Immanuel's veins; "

and still, " even now,"—

> " Sinners, plunged beneath that flood,
> Lose all their guilty stains."

The endless efficacy of the atoning sacrifice is the reason why you may come and believe in Jesus, " even now." If that blood had diminished in its force, I should not dare to speak as I do; but I can, " even now," say with confidence,—

> " Dear dying Lamb, thy precious blood
> Shall never lose its power,
> Till all the ransomed church of God
> Be saved to sin no more."

How many have already entered into glory by the blood of the Lamb! When a man comes to die, nothing else will do for him but this: our own works are a poor staff for us when we pass through the river. All those who are now in the land of light have but one confidence, and but one song: they stand upon the merit of Jesus Christ, and they praise the Lamb who was slain, by whose blood they have been cleansed and sanctified. There is no other way of salvation but that. "Even now" that blood has virtue to take away your sin. Christ is a sufficient Saviour, because his death has unexhausted power. Believe that he can save you "even now."

Again, I would remind you that "even now" is a time of hope to you, because *the Spirit still can renew.* He is yet at work, regenerating and sanctifying. He came down at Pentecost to dwell with his people, and he has never gone back again. He is still in the church. Sometimes we feel his mighty power more than at other times, but he is always at work. Oh, you that do not know anything about the power of the Holy Ghost, let me tell you that this is the most wonderful phenomenon that can ever be observed! Those of us, who have seen and known his mighty energy, can bear testimony to it. In my retirement, at Menton, during the last few weeks, if you had seen me, you would have found me sitting every morning, at half-past nine o'clock, at my little table, with my Bible, just reading a chapter, and offering prayer, my family prayer with the little group of from forty to fifty friends, who daily gathered for that morning act of worship. There they met, and the Spirit of God was manifestly moving among them, converting, cheering, comforting. It was because of no effort of mine; it was simply the Word, attended by the Spirit of God, binding us together, and binding us all to Christ. And here, in this house, for seven-and-thirty years, have I in all simplicity preached this old-fashioned gospel. I have just kept to that one theme; content to know nothing else amongst men; and where are they that have preached new gospels? They have been like the mist upon the mountain's brow. They came, and they have gone. And so it will always be with those who preach anything else but the Word of God; for nothing will abide but the mount itself, the everlasting truth of the gospel to which the Holy Ghost bears witness. That same Holy Ghost is able to give you a new heart "even now", to make you a new creature in Christ Jesus at this moment. Believest thou this?

Once more. I know that "even now" Christ can save you, and I pray you to believe it, for *the Father is still waiting to receive returning prodigals.* Still, as of old, the door is open, and the best robe hangs in the hall, ready to be put upon the shoulders of the son who comes back from the far country, even though he returns reeking with the odour of the swine-trough. How longingly the Father looks along the road, to see whether at length some of you are turning homeward! Ah! did you but know the joy that awaits those who come, and the feast which would load the welcoming table, you would "even now" say, "I will arise, and go to my Father." You should have returned long ago; but blessed be his love, which "even now" waits to clasp you to his heart!

Last of all, *faith is but the work of a moment.* Believe and live. Thou hast nothing to do; thou needest no preparations : come as thou art, without a single plea, but that he bids thee come. Come now, "even now." If Christ were far away, the time that is left to some of you might be too short to reach him; if there were many things which first of all you had to do, your life might close before they were half done; if faith had to grow strong before it received salvation, you might be in the place of eternal despair before your faith had time to be more than a mere mustard seed. But Christ is not far away; he is in our midst, he is by your side. You have nothing to do before you trust him, he has done all; and however weak your faith, if it but comes in contact with Christ, it will convey to you instant blessing. "Even now" you may be saved for ever; for—

> "The moment a sinner believes,
> And trusts in his crucified God,
> His pardon at once he receives,
> Redemption in full, through his blood."

Surely all these are sufficient reasons why "even now" is a time of hope to you; may it also be a time of blessing! It shall be so if thou wilt but at this instant cast thyself on Christ. He says to thee that, if thou wilt but believe, thou shalt see the glory of God. Martha saw that glory. Thou shalt see it too if thou hast like precious faith.

I long that God would give me some souls to-night, on this first occasion when I have met an evening congregation since my return from the sunny South. I desire earnestly that he would set the bells of heaven ringing because sinners have returned, and heirs of glory have been born into the family of grace. I stirred you up to pray this morning. Pray mightily that this word to-night, simple but pointed, may be blessed to many.

Belief, Baptism, Blessing

"And he took them the same hour of the night, and washed their stripes; and was baptized, he and all his, straightway. And when he had brought them into his house, he set meat before them, and rejoiced, believing in God with all his house."—Acts xvi. 33, 34.

THE gospel, attended by the Spirit of God, is always victorious; but it is very pleasant to make notes of its victories. The gospel came to Lydia, a devout woman, who was one given to prayer, and who worshipped God, although she did not know the Lord Jesus Christ. She was a woman of tender heart, and she was soon won. The Lord gently knocked at the door of her heart, and it was opened. She heard Paul's plain preaching, she received the truth, was baptized, and became the corner-stone of the church at Philippi. "Well," says one, "that is an instance of what the gospel does with delicate, tender, gentle natures." Now, here is an old soldier; he has been in the wars, he has earned distinction, and has been appointed to the office of jailor at Philippi, an office of some importance under the Roman Emperor. He is a man who knows the sight of blood; he is of a coarse, though apparently honest, disposition. He keeps prisoners, and that is not an office that brings much gentleness with it; and he is under very stern law. He himself carries out strict discipline in the prison. He is as hard as a bit of the lower millstone. What will the gospel do with him? Brethren, it triumphed as much in the jailor at Philippi as it did in the lady from Thyatira; and while it won its way into the heart of the dealer in purple, it also worked its way into the heart of the dealer in crimson, who had often shed precious blood. The victory over the rough Philippian jailor was as illustrious as the victory over the gentle and devout Lydia.

I want specially to call your attention to this point; the Philippian jailor stands before us as one who was converted, and baptized, and who brought forth useful fruit all in the compass of an hour or so. "Straightway," says my text. It also says, "The same hour of the night." This man was brought from darkness into marvellous light on a sudden; so distinctly brought, that he avowed his conversion there and then, and went on to prove its reality there and then, in his own house, by entertaining the men whom, a few hours before, he had thrust into the inner prison, and whose feet he had made fast in the stocks.

In a great many cases, conversion may be said to be a slow work. I do not think that it really is so; but it appears to be so. There is the early training, there is the awakening of conscience, there is the seeking to find Christ, the struggling, the little light, the dim hope, the faith like a grain of mustard seed, by-and-by a little confidence, afterwards faith more clear, and then, after a long time, comes the public avowal of the joy and peace received through believing. We have a great many people round us who are very slow. Why it is, I do not know; for this is not a slow age. People are fast enough about the things of this world. We cannot travel fast enough. Everything must be done at express speed; but in the things of God there are numbers of persons who are as slow as snails. I have often wondered how the snail got into the ark; he must have started very early to get in. I am thankful that he did get in, however, as certainly as the hare or the gazelle; and many of our crawling friends, I trust, will be found in heaven, and will be really saved, although they are a long while in coming to Christ. It takes a long time to get some of them even a small distance on the road towards a comfortable assurance of salvation.

I have no doubt that the work of grace is very gradual in some people; it is like the sunrise in this country. I am sure that you cannot tell, on foggy mornings, when the sun does rise. I have sometimes questioned whether he ever does rise in England; at all events, I have seen very little of him for the last few days. I believe that the sun has been seen in England; I take it as a matter of trust that that ruddy wafer that I saw the other day really was the sun; although it is a great contrast to the king of day who rules in the sunny South. Who can tell when he begins to shine upon the earth? There is a little grey light, by-and-by a little more, and a little more, and at last you can say that the sun has fairly risen. So it is with some Christians. There is a tiny gleam of light, and then a little more light, and then a further ray of light; but it is only after a considerable time that you can say that the full light has really come into their souls. Yet, mark you, there is a moment when the sun's disc first appears above the horizon. There is a moment when the circle of the sun is really first visible, just an instant, the smallest portion of time; and, in conversion, there must be a time in which death has gone, and life has come; and that must be as sharp a division as the razor's edge could make. There really cannot be anything between life and death. The man is either dead or alive; and there must be some point at which he ceases to be dead, and becomes living. A man cannot be somewhere between condemnation and justification; there is no land in between. The man is either condemned on account of sin, or he is justified through the righteousness of Christ; he cannot be between those two states; so that, after all, in its essence, salvation must be an instantaneous thing. It may be, it will be, surrounded by a good deal that seems to lead up to it, and makes it appear to be gradual; but, in reality, if you get to the root of the matter, there is a turning-point, well-defined and sharp, and if not clear to you, it is clear to the Great Worker, who has wrought in the heart that is changed from death to life, and from condemnation through sin to justification through Jesus Christ.

I. In this Philippian jailor's case, everything is sharp, clear, distinct. In considering it, I will first call your attention to the fact that HERE IS A PERSON CONVERTED AT ONCE.

This man's conversion was wrought at once. *There was no previous thought.* There is nothing that I can imagine in his previous life that led up to it. He had not been plied with sermons, instructions, invitations, entreaties. Probably, up to that night, he had never even heard the name of Jesus Christ; and what he did hear was that these two men, who had come to Philippi preaching Christ, were to be treated with severity, and kept safely. Therefore, he thrust them into the inner dungeon, and made their feet fast in the stocks. All his previous education was un-Christian, if not anti-Christian. All his former life, whatever may have been his Roman virtues, was quite clear of anything like Christian virtue. He knew nothing about that. Nothing could be a greater contrast than the ethics of Rome and the teachings of Christ. This jailor was a good Roman, but he was nothing of a Christian when he thrust the apostles into prison; and yet, before the sun again rose, there was not a better Christian anywhere than that man was. He had passed from death unto life; he was resting on the Christian foundation; he was the possessor of Christian graces. Hear that, ye who have never thought of Christ; and let any man, who came in here to-night a total stranger to true religion, pray that the like may be the case with him, that ere the midnight bell shall toll, he, too, may find the Saviour.

What do you think impressed this man? I think, in part, it may have been *the behaviour of Paul and Silas.* They had no curses on their lips when he made their feet fast in the stocks. They used no ribald language when he thrust them into the innermost cell. They let fall words, I do not doubt, the like of which he had never heard; and their patience, their cheerfulness, their dauntless courage, their holy joy, must all have struck him. They belonged to a different order of prisoners from any he had ever seen before. The jail at Philippi had never held the like of these before, and the jailor could not make them out. He went to bed that night with many thoughts of a new character. Who were these men? Who was this Jesus of whom they spoke?

Then, in the middle of the night, *a singular miracle was wrought.* The prison is shaken by an earthquake. The keeper rises. The prisoners must have gone; for the doors are open. He had not carelessly left them unbolted; he had fastened them before he went to bed; but they are all open, and the prisoners are without chains; they will get away, and he will have to suffer for it. He puts the sword to his own breast; he is about to kill himself, when, just at that moment, he hears a loud voice crying, "Do thyself no harm:

for we are all here." What a surprise for him! What a revulsion of feeling those words caused! "We are all here." He thinks to himself, "Truly there is a God; it must be the God of Paul and Silas who has wrought this miracle." He begins to tremble; he has lived without knowing this God; he has ill-treated the messengers of this God. He brings them out; he respectfully addresses them, "Sirs," he earnestly cries to them, "What must I do to be saved?" The idea of being lost has come over him. It is not that he is afraid to die, for he was about to put himself to death; but he is afraid of what is to follow after death. He is a lost man, and therefore he asks, "What must I do to be saved?"

Now it is that *he is plainly told the way of salvation.* It was put with great brevity, "Believe on the Lord Jesus Christ, and thou shalt be saved, and thy house." Probably he did not understand it when he heard it; and so "they spake unto him the word of the Lord, and to all that were in his house." His wife, his children, his servants, whoever made up his household, all gathered round the two preachers; and they explained the way of salvation, salvation by faith on Christ, salvation by the atoning sacrifice of Christ, salvation by faith in the precious blood of Christ. Paul and Silas doubtless told the company that whosoever believed in Jesus should not perish, but have everlasting life. The jailor believed it, believed every word of it; and he was therefore saved, and saved at once. If you have never heard the gospel before, and you hear it to-night, and believe in Christ, you will be saved at once. If you have been hitherto a total stranger to all good things, yet, if you now receive the blessed tidings of mercy through the Son of God, pardon through his shed blood, you shall go out of this house justified, saved, saved in an instant, saved by the simple act of faith. It is a happy circumstance that the gospel is so simple. There are certain preachers who seem as if they must mystify it, like the negro, who said, "Brethren, I have read you a chapter, and now I will confound it." No doubt there are many who are always making out the gospel to be a very difficult thing to understand; philosophical, deep, and so on; but it was meant for the common people, it was given not merely for the élite, the learned, the instructed, but, "the poor have the gospel preached to them," and the gospel is suitable to be preached to the poor. This is the gospel, "Believe on the Lord Jesus Christ, and thou shalt be saved, and thy house." Trust Christ; and if thou dost, thou shalt be saved.

II. Secondly, HERE IS A PERSON CONFESSING HIS FAITH AT ONCE. "He was baptized, he and all his, straightway."

Should a person be baptized as soon as he believes? As a rule, yes; but there may be good reasons why he should not be. There was no good reason for delay in this man's case, for, in the first place, *his conversion was clear as noonday.* Paul had no question about it. The man was really converted. Silas felt sure of it, too; and they did not hesitate to baptize him and all his household, for they all believed in God. Remember how it was with Philip and the eunuch. That Ethiopian nobleman said, "See, here is water: what doth hinder me to be baptized?" Philip replied, "If thou believest with all thine heart, thou mayest." That being so, they went down both into the water, both Philip and the eunuch, and he baptized him there and then. If the baptizer believes that the professor of faith in Christ is sincere, then he may not hesitate. If he has any doubt about that, if he is afraid that the confession is made in ignorance, or made without due thought, then it may be incumbent upon him to wait a while; but otherwise, he must do as Ananias did to Saul of Tarsus, he must baptize him upon profession of his faith, as soon as he applies. The jailor's conversion, then, was clear.

In his case, also, *there was no other reason for delay.* In the case of many young persons, there are reasons for delay. I remember, in my own case, my parents not believing in the baptism of believers, and I, being between fifteen and sixteen years of age, thought it my duty to consult my father and mother, and ask their counsel and advice. I think I did right; I did not expect them to see with me, but I did expect them to give me their loving concurrence, which they did; and I waited until I had obtained it. Sometimes it will be right on the part of other young people to do the same. There may be reasons, and practical reasons for delay, physical, moral, spiritual; I cannot go into them all at this time. A man may be excusable who, though a believer, is not immediately baptized, seeing that he intends to be as soon as it would be fitting and right and decorous, and, in connection with other duties, a right thing. But there was no reason for delay in the jailor's case. The man was his own master, and his children and his servants had no difficulty in gaining his consent to their baptism, seeing that he himself was about to lead the way in confessing Christ in the Scriptural fashion.

In this man's case, note also, that *he was not hindered by selfish considerations.* Had the jailor been like some people that I know of, he would have found plenty of reasons for delaying his baptism. First, he would have said, "Well, it is the middle of the night. Would you have me baptized at this hour?" He would have said that he did not know that there were conveniences for baptism, for it is so easy to find it inconvenient when you do not like it. He might also have said, "I do not know how the magistrates will like it." He did not care about the magistrates. Perhaps he would lose his situation. He did not take his situation into consideration. Then, what would the soldiers in the Philippian colony say when they heard that the jailor had been baptized into the name of Christ? Oh, the guffaws of the guard-room, the jokes that there would be all over Philippi! This brave man did not take those things into consideration; or if he did, he dismissed them in a moment. It was right for him, now that he believed in Christ, to confess his faith in Christ; and he would do it, and he would do it "straightway." Ah, dear friends, there are some of you here who have never come out as Christians! You are what I call the rats behind the wainscot, or the black beetles that come out at night, when there is nobody about, to get a bit of food, and then go back again. You never say what you are; you never come out on Christ's side. I am not going to condemn you; I wish that you would condemn yourselves, however, for I think that you ought to judge that you are acting a very mean part. The promise of eternal life is not made to a faith which is never avowed.

Allow me to say that over again. The promise of salvation is not made to a faith which is never avowed. "He that believeth and is baptized, shall be saved." "With the heart man believeth unto righteousness; and with the mouth confession is made unto salvation." Our Lord's own words are, "Whosoever therefore shall confess me before men, him will I confess also before my Father which is in heaven;" and he also said, in connection with this confession, "but whosoever shall deny me" (which must mean, whosoever does not confess me) "before men, him will I also deny before my Father which is in heaven." If you have not faith enough in Christ to say that you believe in him, I do not think that you have faith enough in Christ to take you to heaven, for it is written concerning the place of doom, "the fearful", that is, the cowardly, "and unbelieving, shall have their part in the lake which burneth with fire and brimstone."

The fact was, *this man was in downright earnest,* and therefore he would not delay his baptism. He had enlisted in the army of Christ, and he would wear Christ's regimentals straightway. I wish that some who profess conversion, or who profess to desire to be converted, were as much in earnest as this jailor was. "Well," says one, "do not be too severe upon us; I hope that I am a Christian, although I have never confessed Christ yet." Why do you not confess Christ, if you belong to him? I spoke like this to a man who had been, according to his own confession, twenty years a Christian. He had never joined the church; he had never made any open profession of religion; and when I spoke to him, what do you think he said to me? He said, "He that believeth shall not make haste." "Well," I replied, "if you were to be baptized, and to join the church to-morrow morning, I do not think that there would be much haste in it as you have been a believer twenty years; but a much more suitable text for you would be this word of the Psalmist, 'I made haste, and delayed not—to keep thy commandments.'"

"Well," says another, "I have put it off a little while, and————." "A little while!" Is that what you allow your boy to say to you? You say to him, "John, go up into the city for me on an errand." In about an hour afterwards, you see him still at home, and you ask why he has not done your bidding, and he says, "Father, I have put it off a little while." I think it is likely that you would make him recollect that excuse, and not repeat it. But if you were to see him still about the house, hour after hour, and he said to you that he was not disobedient, but he had some little things of his own that he wanted to see to first, I fancy you would teach him what a son's duty is. A servant of that kind would probably have to find a new master very quickly; and do you call yourself a servant of Christ when you have been putting off confessing him by being baptized, putting it off, and putting it off, until, as far as I can see, you are as far off obedience to your Lord's command as ever you were? This jailor, "the same hour of the night" made confession of his faith, "and was baptized, he and all his, straightway," and soon they were all sitting down with Paul and Silas at a love-feast, enjoying happy fellowship with the people of God. Dear friend, if you are converted, do not stand back from confessing Christ. You rob your minister of his wages; for it is his reward to hear that God has blessed your soul. You are also robbing the church. If you have a right to stand out, and not confess Christ, everybody else has the same right; and where would there be any confession of Christ, or any visible church, or any ordinances, or any minister? If you have a right not to come to baptism, and the Lord's Supper, every other Christian has a right to neglect these things also. Then, why were these ordinances instituted at all? What is Christ in his own house? Is he Master, or are you the master; and do you take liberty to do or not do just what you please? Come along, and let my text be true of all of you who believe, "He was baptized, he and all his, straightway."

III. Now, thirdly, HERE IS A PERSON USEFUL AT ONCE. Useful? What could he do?

Well, he did all he could. First, *he performed an act of mercy :* "He took them the same hour of the night, and washed their stripes." Dear, good men, they were covered all over with the marks of the Roman rods. They had been beaten black and blue, and the blood had flowed freely. I think I see how tenderly the jailor washed their stripes. It was before he was baptized that he brought forth fruits meet for repentance. The ill-used ministers needed washing; how could their wounds be healed unless they were properly washed? With all the dust and dirt of the street and the grit of the prison-house in the weals and the wounds, how could they heal? "He washed their stripes." I like to read these words. I am sure Paul and Silas must have enjoyed to have their stripes washed by one who, a little while ago, had been so rough with them. I do not know that he could have done anything better to show his sincere repentance.

He washed their stripes; and when he had done that, and had been baptized, we read that he brought them into his house, and set meat before them. Thus, *he exercised hospitality.* He used his hands and his bath in washing the disciples; now he uses his table, his larder, and his dining-room to entertain them. What more could he do? Seeing that it was the middle of the night, I cannot think of anything more that he could do. So now, if you love the Lord, if you have only just believed in him, begin to do something for him at once. It is a pity that we have so many Christian people, so-called, who do nothing for Christ, literally nothing. They have paid their pew-rent, perhaps; and that is all Christ is to have out of them! He dies for them, redeems them with his precious blood, and they have done nothing for him in return. "I do not know what I could do," says one. I know you could do something. This jailor, within the boundaries of his prison, can do the most needful thing for Paul and Silas; and you, within the boundaries of this house, can do something for Jesus Christ. I would ask you, if you have only to-night believed in Christ, do something for him to-night. By speaking to your wife, or children, or servants, or neighbours, do something for Christ to-night. There is probably no minister shut up in prison in any part of your house, and needing to have his stripes washed. If not, there may be some poor soul somewhere near you that wants a little help. Do an act of charity for Christ's sake. Or there may be some child of God whose heart you could cheer to-night. Do an act of hospitality for some needy saint, and so show your gratitude for what the Lord has done for you. You must do something for Christ if you are a real Christian.

We want to have a church in which all the members do something, in which all do all they can, in which all are always doing all they can, for this is what our Lord deserves to have from a living, loving people bought with his precious blood. If he has saved me, I will serve him for ever and ever; and whatever lies in my power to do for his glory, that it shall be my delight to do, and to do at once. Oh, if some of you get saved to-night, when you get home, there will be a difference in your house! Ah, and within a day or two, even your cat will know that there is a change in you! Everybody in the house will know that you are different from what you were. When a man who has been a drinker gets saved, or one who has been accustomed to use bad language, or one who has given way to passion, or a Sabbath-breaker, or a godless, Christless wretch,—when he gets converted, it is as if hell were turned into heaven, and the devil transformed into an angel. God make it so with any such who are here, by the working of sovereign grace!

I seem, at this moment, to recollect that morning when I found the Saviour. It was a cold snowy morning; and I remember standing before the fire, leaning on the mantel-shelf, after I got home, and my mother spoke to me, and I heard her say outside the door, "There is a change come over Charles." She had not had half-a-dozen words with me; but she saw that I was not what I had been. I had been dull, melancholy, sorrowful, depressed; and when I had looked to Christ, the appearance of my face was changed; I had a smile, a cheerful, happy, contented look at once, and she could see it; and a few words let her know that her melancholy boy had risen out of his despondency, and had become bright and cheerful. May some such change as that pass over you!

IV. Here is one thing more to finish with. Fourthly, HERE IS A PERSON PERFECTLY HAPPY AT ONCE. When the jailor had brought Paul and Silas into his house, "he set meat before them, and rejoiced, believing in God with all his house."

Oh, that was a happy, happy time! "He rejoiced, believing in God with all his house." *He rejoiced that he was saved.* His heart kept beating "Hallelujah! hallelujah! hallelujah!" As he sat at that table with his two strange guests, he had indeed cause for joy. His sin was forgiven; his nature was changed; he had found a Saviour; he had given up his idol gods, and he rejoiced, believing in God. He had been told to believe on the Lord Jesus Christ. He was no Unitarian. He believed Jesus Christ to be God; and he rejoiced, believing in God with all his heart.

And then *he rejoiced that all his household were saved.* What a delight it was to see all his household converted! There was his wife. If she had not been converted, it would have been a very awkward thing for him to have asked Paul and Silas in to that midnight meal. She would have said, "I do not want prisoners coming into my best parlour, and eating up all the cold meat." She would not have liked it; as a prudent housewife, she would have objected to it. But there was Mrs. Jailor waiting on them all with a holy happiness, a new kind of cheerfulness. I do not know whether they had any boys or girls. It may be, or may not be; but however many there were in his household, children or servants, they all believed, "believing in God with all his house." They were all baptized, too, the sons and daughters, and the servants also, for they were included in the household. I do not like it when you count up your household, and leave out Mary Ann, the little servant girl, the last you have had in. You treat her as a drudge; but if she has come into your family, reckon her to be a part of your household; and pray God that they may all be converted—Jane and Mary, your own children, and the other people's children who have come into your houses to do necessary domestic work for you.

The jailor's rejoicing was also *a seal of the Spirit upon his fidelity.* Would it not be delightful for him to sit down with the two preachers of the Word in the middle of the night? Those two men must have had good appetites. They had probably had nothing to eat for many hours, and they had been lying in their dreadful dungeon with their feet in the stocks, after having been cruelly beaten; so they were prepared to eat, whether it was the middle of the night or the middle of the day. And the rest of the family came, and sat down at the table with them, and all rejoiced. Such a night in a prison had never been known before. The jailor "rejoiced, believing in God with all his house."

I think that I heard a friend over there fetch a deep sigh as I quoted those last words of my text. I know what it meant; it meant that he has not all his house converted. Ah, dear brother, I cannot sympathize with you by experience; for I thank God that I have had all my house brought to Christ; but it must be a great sorrow to have that biggest boy of yours acting as he does, or to have that dear girl, of whom you had such bright hopes, turning aside to crooked ways! Let me ask you a question—Have you had faith about your house? Remember that Paul said to the jailor, "Believe on the Lord Jesus Christ, and thou shalt be saved, *and thy house.*" May God give you faith about your house! You have had faith about yourself, and you are saved; exercise faith about your children; cry to God to give you faith about them. Pray believingly that they may be led to have faith for themselves, and so may be saved.

Oh, that all in this great assembly may meet in heaven! You who have heard the Word these many years, may you to-night believe in Christ, and live! You who have never listened to it before, may you also come to Christ, and believe in him, as the jailor did; and like him, you shall be saved! The Lord shall have all the praise and the glory; but oh, that he would work this miracle of mercy to-night! Let us pray for it. Amen.

147